THE JOURNEY OF DACA RECIPIENTS LIVING IN THE UNITED STATES TODAY

A COLLECTION OF PERSONAL STORIES

Introduction

Currently, the United States (USA, here-on-after) is home to hundreds of thousands of individuals who migrated to this country when they were children—often referred to as undocumented youth or "Dreamers." The unique experiences of these migrants (e.g., socialized as "America", while also holding a legally vulnerable and liminal status) propelled their advocacy to demand for rights (e.g., employment authorization) that would enable their success in USA—a capitalistic environment where limited access to basic rights equates a life-sentence of poverty, discrimination, and challenges. In turn, many of those undocumented youth obtained.

Deferred Action*, the ability to *legally* live and work here temporarily. This executive order allowed for them to live without fear of immediate deportation. Many of these individuals had bachelors and masters degrees, but until then, were not able to pursue careers due to not having a valid social security number. Ultimately, although not a permanent or humane order, DACA (Deferred Action for Childhood Arrivals), allowed hundreds of thousands of young undocumented professional to utilize their degrees and work as educators (e.g., teachers, professors), computer programmers, accountants, health professionals (e.g., nurses, doctors, paramedics), etc. More than a decade later, the debate continues in Washington as to whether or not these "Dreamers," as they were labeled, deserve to become citizens of this country.

Between 2012 and 2016, over 700,000 individuals were able to obtain DACA, which exponentially improved their lives. In 2021, the opportunity was given for hundreds of thousands more to apply for this benefit, but due to a lawsuit in federal court, their paperwork was never processed.

Although evidence indicates that migrants, legally vulnerable and otherwise, greatly contribute to the USA, for decades now, politicians have used legally vulnerable migrants—undocumented young people and refugees/asylum seekers—as tokens. These politicians often speak for migrants without listening to migrants' reasons for migration and future goals. Instead of listening, both major parties blame each other for not passing legislation that would provide citizenship to millions of individuals who illegally came to the USA as children. However, when it comes to garner votes from the Latine community, politicians abuse their understanding of the legal system to exploit migrants' traumatic experiences as fundraising opportunities for their campaigns; once elected, unfortunately, these politicians do little to support the migrants they used as objects to climb USA's political ladder.

It is imperative that we go beyond listening to politicians' narratives of DACA recipients. Instead, we should turn to migrants who have experienced immigration challenges. As such, this book is authored by several DACA recipients who share their stories of migration, including describing challenges they faced in order to achieve their goals. All these authors

3

earned a bachelors or masters degree, and one is currently pursuing a doctorate in medicine. We recognize that not all DACA recipients need to pursue a college diploma because this country needs workers in various economic areas. Our goal in choosing these specific individuals is to provide insights on their unique experiences.

This project was initiated with fifteen individuals; eight were able to complete their writing. Some of them became overwhelmed with memories of trauma, discrimination, and loss. Those who completed their writing have much more to say, but recognize that if they kept writing, each one of them could write a multivolume collection of stories.

Once you have read about their experiences, we hope your understanding of legally vulnerable migrants will positively change—we also hope you become an ally who advocates for a resolution, policy, or law that provides more than what DACA currently offers, temporary reprieve. By all intents and purposes, this is their country—it is a piece of paper and a nine (9) digit number that excludes their social participation in a country they help build.

*Deferred Action refers to undocumented individuals who arrived to the USA prior to age 16 and prior to June 15, 2007 and who could demonstrate that they have been continuously living in the country since then. Those who qualified are required to reapply every two years to renew their permit to legally live and be able to work in the country. The cost of the application is over $500 each time and does not cost taxpayers a dime. The program was stopped in 2016 due to a lawsuit and hundreds of thousands of others who could have qualified applied, but were left in limbo. To this day, their applications are stalled.

Resilience

by Alex Martinez

You rang the church bells of freedom;
You preached justice and equality;
You told stories of a great dream;

We listened;
We climbed mountains
We crossed deserts and oceans
We swam across rivers
to get to this dream.

We press on;

But when we arrived
we were met with
Hostility,
Anger, and
Racism.

We press on;

We pick your food
We built your bridges and roads
We teach your children,
We nurse your elders,
But we are still not welcome.

We press on;

The dream you preached
was a lie;
You were a lie.

We sacrificed it all
Our family,
Our community,
Our home,
For your lie

All we can do now
is hope that our offspring will
Rise
like resilient redwoods
Rise
like powerful waves
Rise
like courageous lions.

So we will
keep pressing on

For our dreams,
For our family,
For our people,

For ourselves!

Brayan Araiza

The Divided States of America means a country of opportunities and struggles as a person of color. Growing up in this country, the opportunities are earned while the struggles come in a variety of ways whether it is to simulate to try to fit in or whether you are too "white washed" to be considered Mexican. Growing up in a predominantly white wealthy town I have learned to be proud of my culture, family, and beliefs. I am also thankful for my parents sacrificing everything to give my brother, sisters, and I a better life and a brighter future.

I was born in Mexico City, also known as el D.F. in Ecatepec de Morelos on April 26, 1992. Growing up I spent a lot of time in the colonia de Obrera Jajalpa, that is a town/colony named Obrera Jajalpa within the state of Mexico City. That is where majority of my family resided that included my parent's extended family such as, their parents, siblings, cousins, aunt/uncles and other relatives. Due to the vast population in Mexico City, colonias are like towns within the city. We lived in the poorest parts of the city where the homes are small and made up of cement. One street can have up to 50 homes, thus you get to know a lot of people and have close knit communities within your street. The street we lived in had a curbside while the other side of the street did not. No matter where you live there is. Store nearby which meant easy access to any need such as food, cleaning supplies, or any household item. In addition, someone nearby no matter where you lived sold a dish such as, tamales, which my grandma did, tlacoyos, tacos, huaraches, pambazos, etc. I am proud of where I was born and have the fondest memories of living in my colonia.

I migrated to this country when I was eight years old. My father lost his well-paying job in Mexico. He worked in a factory as a manufacturing technician. I remember his schedule changed from week to week working during the days for a week and then working at nights the following week. My favorite schedule is when he would work early in the mornings, which meant he would be home in the evenings to hang out with my brother and I. One of my favorite memories with my dad is teaching me how to ride a bike. In the Colonia/Town we lived in there were multiple canchas (courts), that were at the center of the colonia. He would take me there in the evenings in my blue bike and encourage me to continue to practice how to ride a bike without my training wheels. In the middle of all the canchas there was a huge light pole that I would gravitate to like two magnets coming together. I did not understand why I would keep running into that pole. We would move far away from it and somehow I would find my way crashing into it. I hit that pole with my bike so many times that my father could not contain his laughter. Looking back at it now, I am so thankful for him teaching me how to ride a bike because he did not give up on me until I figured it out. His persistence, dedication, and perseverance towards me is something I would continue to see, as we migrated to the United

States of America. My father lost his job because the factory was moving to another part of Mexico and he would need to take a pay cut. This was something my father could not afford to survive providing for a family of four. After my father realized that he could not follow his job to provide for our family he and my mom decided that my dad would come to the United States of America to save enough money to buy a house or finish paying for the apartment he was buying. He then would return to Mexico to find a new job to provide for our family. I remember my parents telling me that my dad would miss my 8th birthday, which I did not take well and would not understand their decision. As a child I was a lot more emotional than I am now, as an adult, and I wonder as I am writing this if this is where I began suppressing my emotions to be strong for our family. I remember my dad telling me, "regresare pronto y te podre comprar lo que tu quieras". I believed him as my dad always kept his word. After he left, everything would change. For some reason I do not recall this part of my childhood but my mom has described that I was not acting the same after he left. I was more irritable, angry, frustrated and would regularly ask about when dad would be home. She even said I would wake up crying in the middle of the night looking for my dad. From what I can remember, I did not feel safe and was never happy as if it was ripped away. It got to the point where I would need to sleep with my mom and brother in the same bed. On my 8th birthday I remember talking to my dad on the phone and asking him, "cuando regresaras?", as he replied, "regresare pronto" "I will return soon". As time went by, I got worse according to my mom, since I do not recall this part of my childhood. A few weeks went by and I continued to sleep with my mom and brother on the same bed. It got to the point where she moved her bed into the living room because I would sleep walk or wake up yelling in tears. Until one day, my mother approached us asking us if we wanted to see our dad soon. I immediately thought that we could finally be together again, excitement and relief rushed my body that he would be home. That is when my mom told us we would be going to where he was at, "Los Estados Unidos". At first, I was overjoyed thinking about seeing my dad and began counting down the days I would get to see him. My mother began selling our stuff and giving away some of our things to family. Everything she cherished was placed into the apartment that my dad was paying off. My uncle would end up living there with his family. As the day got closer to leaving, I started to realize that I was leaving everything and everyone I knew for some time, is what I believed at the time. My mom explained that we would be going with dad for some time and then we would all return together after he had saved enough money to pay for the apartment he was purchasing. She further explained that in "Los Estados Unidos", my dad would be able to save money to finish paying for the apartment and give him enough time to find a new job back in Mexico. I acted as if I understood but all I kept thinking about was the fact that I would see my dad and be able to have our family back together.

Looking back at it now, I believe that was my mom and dad's intentions, but as time went by living in this country. My parents realized that they could provide a lot more, and that my brother and I would have a lot more opportunities to be successful. I believe their intentions changed the longer we stayed in this county. In Mexico, I would hear stories of how people threw away brand new stuff such as televisions, toys, furniture, bikes, clothes, and much more. The streets were so clean that you could find money on the ground. Everyone lived in big houses and had multiple cars. People had nice clothes and kids did not have to wear a uniform to school. I would come to find out all the stories were lies or exaggerated truths.

The migration process was a terrifying, unpredictable, chilling voyage. Although I had a level of excitement as an eight-year-old boy getting to see his dad again, I can recall many aspects of the process. From getting into a plane for the first time and realizing that I was leaving everything I knew and everyone I loved, specifically my uncle "Nicho" is a day I can recall, as if it was yesterday. I remember my mom saying, "párate hijo nos tenemos que ir", "wake up son we need to leave", I remember looking outside and telling my mom it is still night and she replied, "vamos a ver a papa", "we will go see dad". I remember grabbing the backpack that my mom packed for all of us with some clothes and Pokemon cards that she allowed me to bring. As we headed to the airport, my mom was carrying my brother as he continued to sleep in her arms. He was six years old at that time and she could still carry him, as I was too heavy for her. I could not go back to sleep due to the excitement of seeing my dad again. I look over at my mom and uncle, "Nicho" . They do not share my excitement or happiness instead; their faces display doubts, fears, uncertainties, and suspicions. As we arrive at the airport, I see tears tumble from my uncle's face. This was the first time seeing him cry which I could not understand why he was so sad. As he understood, the reality of us moving to a different country would change our family. He tells me, "te quiero mucho y cuidas a tu mama y a tu hermano", "I love you so much and take care of your mom and brother". I begin to cry asking him to come with us not realizing the journey we were about to embark on. That would be the last time I would give my uncle a hug. We got on the plane and I remember being happy, nervous, and anxious because I was going to see my dad while leaving my uncle and everything I knew behind, **with a feeling that I would come back and everything would go back to normal**. Before landing, I remember my mom giving me a list of do's and don'ts: Stay close to me, keep your brother close to you, be strong, you are the leader and the man to take care of us, act normal, and follow all my orders. Do not ask questions, do not run around, do not ask for food, and do not cry. As the plane takes off, I get a head rush, as if I were riding in a roller coaster at la feria. I look over at my mom and her eyes are trying to hold back tears, holding my brother's hand as he sleeps. I can tell she wants to show a strong face but her emotions are overwhelming her and she is also scared as this is her first time on a plane as well. As I stare at my mom, I realize this is not a normal trip and it would alter our lives. We arrive at our destination in the middle of the day. We headed outside the airport; a man was waiting for us as I followed my mom's dos and don'ts, showing strength in my face while being scared and apprehensive inside. I remember stepping outside feeling a wave of heat that I had never experienced before that dried my mouth instantly. I remember wanting to ask my mom for water but I wanted to stay quiet and strong in order to get to see my dad. We got in this strangers car as he made small talk with my mom while I distracted my six-year-old brother trying to figure out where we were. I ask my mom "donde estamos?", "where are we?", she replies, "Mexicali" and reminds me to just follow her and do as she says and not ask any more questions. I kept wondering if this man was taking us to my dad? Or is my dad living here because I do not like how hot it is here. We arrived at this man's house and he discloses he lives here with his mother. The man leads us to a bedroom where he tells my mom that my brother and I can stay in the room as she will stay in a different room. The room becomes tense as if we were in a steam room making it hard to breathe. I freeze not knowing what to do or say. My mom aggressively responds "yo me quedo con mis hijos", "I stay with my children". My mom shows a strong face, but I can sense her fear of us sleeping apart in this unknown place. Luckily, her strength and assertiveness breaks the room's tension. They go back and forth until the man ceases to my mom. I was so scared because this man was larger than I was and their back and forth made me realize how powerless I was, as an 8 year old boy. She then explains we will be staying here until tomorrow night, so many questions flooded my mind. Where is my dad? Why are we here? Who was that man? I wish I had water. I keep wondering if this man is going to return and split us up. I was distracted by the heat, it felt like we were in a sauna. My mom explained to my brother and I, "nos quedaremos aquí hasta mañana en la noche". I don't recall spending the first day in the room. My mom explains that we just waited in the room as my brother and I entertained ourselves quietly playing with our hands as toys. As the night approached my brother fell asleep, I tried my hardest to stay awake fearing that the man would return; but eventually the heat exhausted me to sleep. I ask my mom about the first night of our journey, and she discloses that she did not sleep that night protecting my brother and I. As she also worried about the man entering the room while we slept. The following day I woke up in a panic looking for my mom and brother as she told me, "aqui estoy no te preocupes", "I am here don't worry". I ask her, "donde esta mi papa", she replies, "estaremos con él pronto". She then explains to my brother and I that we will be staying in this room again until the night. I don't recall spending two full days locked in a room as I believe I blocked that from my mind. Although I can vividly remember the night we spent there and the night we left. I do not recall what we did or even if we ate while we were locked in the room. My mom clarifies that the strange man brought one meal each day that consisted of three burgers from McDonalds. That would be the first time I would eat a burger but both meals are a fog in my mind. Although I do not recall spending two days locked in a room, as the night of our departure arrived so due my memories. The man knocks on the door and lets himself before my mom can reply. He tells my mom it is time to go. My mother once again grabs my brother as he sleeps and tells me to follow her into this man's car once again. We drive through the night as I am somewhat awake wondering where will we end up now and when is this going to end? I look over at my mom and I can tell she is scared and worried like something bad is about to happen. I tell myself I will protect them as Goku protects his family. As I am writing my story I realize how much the journey changed me and shaped the man I am today. I don't recall how far we went as I fell asleep until I heard my mom desperately tell me "despiertate ya nos vamos". The man stopped at a shopping center and told us to get out as they are here to pick you guys up. My sleepiness vanishes in an instant as I get out of the car, while my mother carries my sleepy brother in her arms. Two women approach us and they ask my mom her name and she replies, "Veronica". The women then ask us to follow them and request that she wake my brother up. We arrive at their car as they begin telling my mom that my brother and I will go with one of them and my mom will go with the other. I notice my mom get apprehensive as she replies, "esto no era el plan", "this was not the plan". One of the women replies, "This was not the plan but if you want to go through your kids will need to go with her". I can not imagine being in this position as I am a father now. This must have been one of the hardest decisions my mother had to make as the plans had changed. I see her look at us as my brother is sleepy not realizing what was happening, Although I do not blame him as he was only six years old. I am fully awake realizing the situation at hand, she gets on one knee and gets close to my face and she tells me, "cuidas a tu hermano y siempre se quedan juntos", I nod. There was so much I wanted to tell her but I was frozen in fear trying to give her some level of comfort that I would take care of my brother and that I was not scared. The woman tells us to get in the car, she will take us to see our dad. Without a hesitation my brother hops in the car. Before I get in the car I look at my mom and ask her "tu estaras bien?" She replies, "si, le haces caso a la señora y cuidas a tu hermano". As her voice cracks and trembles as she is trusting a strange woman to take her kids. We enter the car and the woman tells us "todo estara bien, quieren ir al McDonalds", she asks, my brother replies, "si" with excitement as this would be the first time going to a McDonalds restaurant. We had heard about how they have a playground in the restaurant which we always wanted to go to but could not afford it. This would be my first memory of eating and going to a McDonalds, although I do not recall the other two times I had eaten a burger when we were locked in the room. To this day I wonder why I do not recall the two days being locked in a room and eating two burgers which is all we were given to eat. We drive away as I try to look where my mom went but I could not see because it was dark out and the woman sees that I am looking for my mom and tells me to sit down and look forward. We drive for about 10 minutes until we get to a bridge with each lane having a little hut with an officer inside and several officers outside checking people before letting them go through. I now know they were immigration officers. Since it was so late there were not a lot of people trying to cross the bridge. As we get closer and closer to the check point my brother tells me, "mira alla esta el McDonalds", I reply, "si pero ya no digas nada". The lady then shushes us and tells us not to say a word. As we arrive at the hut the officer begins to talk to the woman and request documentation. As the woman hands the officer three little booklets, which I now know were passports. Two other officers begin to walk around the car, while one is holding a dog and bringing it close to the car. I vividly remember being so scared feeling that we were doing something wrong even though I was just trying to have our family together. The officer continues to question the woman but she is speaking with authority and confidence, as she explains that we are her nephews and that she is taking us back to our parents from our vacation. The officer seems hesitant to believe her as he continues to ask her other questions. The longer we sit there the more nervous the woman is getting and the more I worry that we are about to get arrested. I look over to hold my brother's hand

and he surprisingly asks the woman, "cuando vamos allegar al McDonalds, tengo hambre?". We can see the McDonalds from the checkpoint but I did not expect him to talk because we were told not to. Everyone was surprised as the air was getting thick and heavy from the back and forth between the officer and the woman. His question broke the tension between the officer and woman because he then told the woman "ya se pueden ir, ese nino tiene hambre". I was mad, happy, scared, and relieved that he let us go through because the woman was starting to run out of confidence. We continue to drive and the woman nervously tells my brother, "ya vamos a comer hijo", with relief in her voice. We entered the McDonalds. I look around hoping to see my mom. The woman notices and tells me not to worry as she will be with us soon and to stop looking around. The woman buys us two happy meals and takes us to a table. My brother cannot hold back his excitement as he knows there is a toy in the happy meal. She hands my brother his box first and before she can hand me mine, his box is opened and showing me his toy. I fake my excitement as I look out the window hoping to see my mom arriving but there is no car in sight. I can see other cars going through the checkpoint as we did hoping that my mom is in one of those cars coming to get us. Once again, the woman notices that I am looking around and not eating as she firmly tells me to stop looking around because that can get us in trouble including your mom. I am immediately terrified and begin to eat. My brother asks the woman if we can go play in the indoor park as she replies, "no, acaba tu comida por que no podras llevartela". I tell him, "comete todo", understanding that we do not know when our next meal will come. I notice a car drive into the parking lot giving me hope that my mom is in it but it quickly vanishes into the night. We continue to eat as I focus on eating as fast as I can thinking if we finish our food faster we will get to see our mom. My brother is so distracted playing with his toy that he is neglecting his food. I tell him to eat all of his food and I'll let him play with my toy as well. He listens and begins gulping down his food remembering that he was hungry. As I am eating, I think to myself, what will I do if this woman does not take us back to our mom. I play various scenarios in my head and look over to my brother as he eats, I promise myself "lo protegere con mi vida". As I continue to think, I realize I did not see my mom get into a car at the shopping center we separated from, I did not know if my mom would be coming here to meet us or will we be taken to her. My mind kept thinking of every situation possible and how the night would end. I am in my own head and don't realize my mom walking in with two women into the McDonalds, while my brother loudly screams, "mama ve mi juguete", she replies, "no grites, esta bonito". I felt lighter when I saw my mom and my immediate reaction was to ask her if she was okay. Knowing she had gotten through the same checkpoint we did. She replied, "estoy bien, no te preocupes", as she held my hand I noticed her hand was sweaty which I concluded that she was just as frightened as I was at the checkpoint. The relief I felt seeing my mom quickly vanished as we were told we were going with another man to a different house for the night. The women tell the man, "our job is done", and tell my mom, "buena suerte". That phrase made me more frightened, as if we were about to go through something more difficult, I did not expect our journey to go this way. I thought this is why my uncle was crying realizing the danger we were in. The man took us to a house, I was not sure if it was his or not, as my mind goes into a fog again, until we arrive at the house. We were taken to a room with a small bed as my mom and brother quickly fell asleep. The adrenaline from the encounter with the officers kept me up. My mom must have been exhausted, as she had not slept very much from the night before. I laid in bed thinking, is this what my dad went through? Will we be okay? And how long will this last? I laid there looking at the ceiling until I faded into sleep. The following day, we are woken with a knock on our door with the man telling us it is time. My mom woke up surprisingly as she was in deep sleep realizing she had slept in. The knock also woke me up but I woke up determined and ready for whatever came at us. It was a weird confidence with a looming fear. My mom wakes my brother up but he does not want to wake up and she says, "vamos ir con papa". This time I knew better and was not going to believe it until I saw it. We head out of the room as I offer my mom to carry the backpack, she declines. This time I noticed the sun was out and there was daylight around noon, which meant we had slept in. The man introduces us to a man and woman, I am assuming they are a couple. They ask us to follow them outside to their car. The woman begins to explain that we will be driving for a while as she opens the back door. She proceeds to pull out a hidden small string from the back seat crevice between the door and top part of the back seat. Explaining that when you pull it the entire back seat rest pulls up into the trunk. I thought to myself, why is this relevant? She says, "los tres entraron dentro de la cajuela cuando les digamos y no hagan ruido", " the three of you will enter the trunk when we tell you to and do not make noises". I looked at my mom and her response was, "estaremos bien", she read my face. I was shocked and horrified. She further explains how we will fit in the trunk. My mom will enter first on her side making a "C" shape with her body, then my brother will follow, and I will be the last one to enter. They also tell us they will not be able to stop, thus, we will need to enter the trunk while they are driving. The woman also apologizes as their AC does not work and it will be a long hot ride. It was sunny out but it was not super hot, so we entered the car and headed out. As we drive I see nothing but desert and mountains in the distance. My brother quickly falls asleep, I look over at my mom and she tells me, "duermete un rato". I respond "no tengo sueno", but within an hour I fall asleep. I don't know how long I've slept but the heat wakes me up with sweat dripping down my neck. I look over at my brother and mom and he is playing with the McDonalds toys and she has a red face from the heat. My mom tells me to take off my sweater as she also notices that I am sweating a lot. The drive seemed endless with nothing but desert and heat. They rolled down their windows and the wind was so hot it felt like a heater was hitting my face. I don't know what was better, the closed windows with trapped heat or hot air hitting my face. The moment finally came with the woman directing us to get in the trunk. My mother quickly responded by opening up the backseats and getting in. She pulled my brother in close to her as I followed. I did not think I would miss sitting in the hot air, because the trunk was hotter. The woman puts a blanket over the back seats covering the open gap from the missing backseat. She reminded us to be quiet, my throat was completely dried and I recall being so thirsty I could chug an entire gallon of water. My mom whispers, "esta bien", my brother responds, "tengo sed". I feel her move around as she is getting him a water bottle. I am not facing them, thus I don't know when and how she had a water bottle. All I can see is the thick Mexican blanket that the woman had put over the back seats. I hear him drinking the water while she whispers, "no te la tomes toda". I was so uncomfortably hot on my side just feeling my shirt slowly get wet as I cannot stop sweating. The woman checks in on us every 10 minutes or so asking if we are okay. My mom hands me the water over my shoulder and I see that it is less than half full. I assumed my brother had drank a lot of it which was understandable because we were inside of a trunk in the middle of the desert. I put the water over my shoulder and whisper, "no tengo sed", she insists that I need to drink some. I open the bottle and take a small sip understanding that my brother will ask for more and my mom will also need some. My mom constantly asks me and my brother if we are okay. Every time she asks us if we are okay my brother asks, "ya mero llegamos" and every time she responds, "si un poco mas". It felt an eternity being confined in a trunk feeling like we were inside of an oven. I feel the car begin to slow down and the woman tells us to be quiet and not move around. I immediately think this must be another check point. We come to a complete stop and the man begins talking to another man, which I am assuming is an officer. I stare into the blanket not moving a muscle, as I clasp my hands together hoping everything goes well. I hear them speaking a language I do not understand. I also hear them laughing thinking this is a good thing but also feeling upset having to endure this heat. I hear someone walking outside around the car as I squeeze my hand tighter hoping my mom is okay and my brother doesn't say anything. I don't recall how long we stopped but I finally felt the car move. I am stuck in the same position I don't know for how long until I hear the woman say, "estan bien, todavía no pueden salir, un poco mas". As I continue to stare into the blanket. I hear my mom asking my brother if he is okay and there is no response. I feel her panic as she lightly shakes him. I instantly panic but there is nothing I can do. He finally responds, "tengo sed" as she gives him more water. I hear him drinking the water, being relieved that he is okay. He tells her, "tengo mucho calor ma", all she can respond is, "ya mero". Hearing her talk about her experience, explaining how she was worried about him overheating and passing out has given me a greater insight of the love and sacrifice she had to make to give us a better life. She then asks me if I am okay and if I want water? Again I tell her I am okay and that I am not thirsty. Although, I can feel my lips cracking from the dryness of my mouth and the excruciating heat. I continue to be strong to be one less worry for my mom as she is constantly shaking my brother making sure he is okay. Time went by so slow but I kept thinking of all the great memories I had with my dad. As I was fading into sleep I heard the woman say, "ya pueden salir", "you guys can come out". I was glad to be able to get out. I can tell the women looked at me with a worried face as I was bright red with my shirt drenched with sweat. I look at my mom and brother and they look the same, I ask if they are okay and my mom says, "toma agua". I tell her you first as she finally takes a sip of water. She handed it over to me and I took a small sip of water too and the water was so warm it felt like I was drinking tea. My brother finishes it off and the woman says, "todavía falta para llegar a Los Ángeles pero ya pasamos", "we still have some time to get to Los Angeles but we have passed". I did not know how long we were in the trunk but my mom estimates we were in there for 2 hours which were the 2 longest hours of my life. We finally begin to see a city, while I look around and all I can think of is a whole new world from what I was accustomed to. It was the first time I was seeing huge buildings and big houses and I thought "ya estamos en los Estados Unidos". The woman begins to explain to us that when we see my dad not to run, show excitement, or make a scene because we were still in danger of being arrested. Again, I told myself, "I won't believe it until I see it". We arrive at a parking lot and I see my dad standing outside of a car. I wanted to cry and tell him everything we had just gotten through but I remembered to stay cool, calm and collective as we were still in danger. The woman tells my mom, "get out and walk your kids over to him holding their hand". My mother thanks the couple and tells us to thank them as well. We both say "gracias" and she replies, "que dios los bendiga". We walk over to my dad and he grabs my head as he tells me to get in the car with my brother. My mother gives him a kiss and gets in the car. I was finally relieved that we were all together but this was just the beginning of my life changing forever.

Adapting to this new culture and language was extremely difficult but very necessary in order to help my family restart our lives. As the eldest child, there was a level of expectation and pressure to help my family navigate this new world. My dad had a job where he worked as many hours as he could to provide for our family. Which meant he was hardly ever home and when he was, he was so tired to spend quality time with my brother and I. When I was younger, I did not understand why our family dynamic had changed, but as I noticed my dad leaving super early to work on a bike and coming home when it was dark. I began to despise this country. I went from knowing everyone and understanding everything someone said to not knowing anything and not having friends but my brother and cousin. Adapting to the "American" culture was harder for me than it was for my brother. We now talk about it and he hardly has memories of our life in Mexico that makes me feel mad and glad for him because he did not feel alone nor an outcast as I did, when we first arrived in this country. In Mexico, people are always outside and friendly from my memories as a child. When we got to the U.S., it felt like no one ever went out and if people did it felt like they would look at us with weird looks. The "American" culture seems colder, standoffish, distant, something I did not understand because Mexican culture is all about warmth, togetherness, and collaboration. Furthermore, in Mexico I loved going to school. I was a good student and had many friends. When I first attended school here in the U.S. is a memory I will never forget. I was the new kid in school that could not speak English and felt like other kids looked at me as if I came from another planet. English sounded so strange to me but I knew I had to learn it to help my family. My first day of school I was introduced to the entire class. I felt so embarrassed because I did not understand what anyone was saying and it felt like I was being laughed at. I was given flashcards of simple words with pictures on them and was told to go over them for the entire day. The teacher was only able to sit with me for about an hour teaching me how to pronounce the words that were on the cards such as, car, house, mouse, fence, etc. Another strategy that helped me learn the language was playing memory cards where you shuffle all the cards and lay face down. You then turn around two cards face up until you find the match. I enjoyed playing that game because there was a memory factor that began helping me learn the words and connecting them with the pictures. I began trying to absorb as much information as I could in order to help my family. Furthermore, the biggest strategy I used to learn English was watching cartoons such as, Dragon Ball Z, Power Rangers, and others that I had memorized watching them in Mexico and I understood what they were saying. Listening to the cartoons in English was an adjustment but I understood the dialog in Spanish and began connecting the dots while I heard them in English. In addition, once I knew what a word meant I pronounced it in my head and out loud over and over again in order for it to sound perfect in English. By 5th grade, I became fluent in English. It was the hardest thing I had ever done because I worked so diligently to master the language and sound like my peers did.

It has been a long time since I have been in Mexico. What I miss the most is the food and the holiday celebrations that are different from the United States. Although the United States has Mexican food, it does not compare to food in Mexico. My favorite dish is el pambazo that consists of torta bread dipped in a homemade red sauce. Then the bread is fried in a pan on both sides until it is crispy on the outside and soft on the inside. It has chorizo and potatoes smashed together. The chorizo and potatoes are spread on the inside of the bread and you add Mexican cheese, lettuce, sour cream and salsa. Other Mexican dishes that I miss that are rare to find here in the United States and even if they are found they do not taste the same are, Tlacoyos, tacos de canasta, and tamales oaxaquenos. The celebrations in Mexico are very different then they are here in the United States. For example, Christmas in Mexico is celebrated on December 24. In our family, we did an exchange, which meant everyone would get one gift. A couple weeks prior to Christmas the adults would get together and write everyone's name on a small piece of paper and everyone would then pick a piece of paper out of a cup for the exchange. My grandfather would make a fogata (bonfire) in this huge metal container and he would place it outside of his house where everyone would sit around. People would eat, share stories, drink, and play games. Although the fogata was meant for our family, neighbors and friends would trickle in on the festivities as the celebration progressed. At midnight we would do the exchange and one by one they would reveal who they picked for the exchange and give them their gift. Everyone would always clap and encourage the person to open their gift by chanting, "que lo abra, que lo abra". Everyone witnessed you open your gift and give your gift to your person. That was one of my favorite parts because there was excitement for you to get your gift and thrill for you to give your person their gift. It was more about the activity than the actual gift. At Christmas, we would also play with fireworks. My dad would buy my brother and I a huge black bag of all types of fireworks, big ones, loud ones, bright ones, and explosive ones.

Now that I am a lot older, I have not considered moving from the U.S.A because the majority of my family now resides in this county. On the other hand, I do have an uncle in Mexico that I have not seen since I was eight years old. He is another father figure I have that I can only talk to via phone and now see via FaceTime due to the advances of technology. I remember my uncle "Nicho" being a gentle giant, who always allowed me in his room and would always give me soda even though my mom would not be okay with that. He would always converse with me about any topic I chose and would always give me a peso or money to buy candy at the nearby "tienda". He would always take time to hang out with me as he would be one of my favorite people to be around. Lastly, I chose to stay here in this country because I also have a family of my own now that includes my wife and one-year-old son who I love.

In conclusion, the best advice I would give another immigrant who is going through the immigration process is to forge forward. To never lose hope and continue to learn and grow and break the institutional trauma that many of us have within our families. To understand the sacrifices our parents and/or ourselves have made for a better life. While also living in the present and letting go of all the fears we carry as immigrants to a country that does not accept us. Yet, we are striving, thriving, and making a change throughout all communities in this country. To help uplift one another and fight injustices that many of us have faced through our life.

Jorge Hurtado

In the writing of this chapter, I have omitted to write about some personal topics at this time. I have written this chapter in hope that readers can relate to some of my experiences and are encouraged to pursue their dreams.

What does the following mean to you: "The Divided States of America"?

It means the historical and ever-increasing division in the U.S. in terms of human rights, systemic racism, income/education inequality, health inequities, political views and ultimately values. Personally, I consider myself a Californian. I am grateful to have lived most of my life in the state of California, which is not perfect and has many things to improve, but ultimately it is a state that has given me and many others the opportunity to an education, healthcare, a driver's license, and more. Thanks to living in this state and the California Dream Act, I have had access to higher education that I may not have had in other states or even in my home country. In Mexico, access to a university or a professional degree would not have been possible for me given the little government support for students. Until recent years, only grades K-9th were guaranteed by the Mexican federal government, it was only in 2012 that grades 10th -12th became compulsory.[2] Financial support for college/higher education is very limited to students as opposed to here in California. Additionally, in the state of California, community college is free and there is financial aid available for undocumented and Deferred Action for Childhood Arrivals (DACA) students in the form of the California Dream Act which essentially supports students who do not qualify for Free Application for Federal Student Aid (FAFSA) up to their Bachelor's degree. Living in California has been like living in a bubble of opportunity, diversity, better access to healthcare, and progressiveness.

When and where were you born?

I was born in *Tierra Caliente (hot land)* otherwise known as Apatzingán, Michoacan, Mexico in 1993. I grew up with *mis abuelitos (my grandparents)* and one of my three sisters, M. I am the youngest of four. My other two sisters, J & L moved to the U.S. when they turned 18 since they are U.S. citizens. My sister M, my abuelitos and I lived in a rural area at the outskirts of the town and struggled to make ends meet. We depended on my grandfather's income as a farmworker. Every day, he got up at 3am to pick cucumber or limes in the fields to make sure we had something to eat. At around the age of 8, I remember asking him to bring me with him to help, but he never allowed me in hopes that I would go to school and have a better opportunity. I recall waking up in the morning sad and disappointed that he didn't wake me up to join him. At the age of 12, during the weekends, I started working picking up limes and understood the hard work that is working in the fields. I realized then the great sacrifices that my grandfather and my grandmother made for me and my sister.

I went to a school with very limited resources, my elementary school only had 3 classrooms for grades 1-6. My lunch money consisted of 3 pesos or about 15 U.S. cents, but despite our financial challenges I managed to be a bright student. Through elementary school, I received good grades, and even represented my elementary school in the 6th grade in a regional academic competition. Through my education in the U.S., I learned that the part of our brain called the amygdala is very keen at remembering traumatic situations. I recall having to walk to school every day fearful of being chased and attacked by dogs along the way. This of course occurred more than once. On one occasion, as I walked to school, a large Pitbull jumped the fence of its home to attack me. I waited there completely paralyzed as I called for its owner to come out. The owner did not come out soon enough, so I ran for it, fell and got mud all over. I kept walking while crying because I had to get to school. This is a good example of how trauma works and how traumatic experiences can change us for the rest of our lives. This and other similar experiences caused me to develop a fear of dogs from a young age. Over the years, very loving dogs changed my developed fear for them. By allowing myself to address my trauma, I discovered how loving our furry friends truly are. I use this anecdote to highlight the hold trauma can have in our lives, but with work and courage, we can heal from it.

One of my older sisters, J, who was born in the U.S. and lived there since the age of eighteen, supported us financially after my grandfather was unable to continue working due to old age. She would travel back and forth and bring us clothes and other things, which to us who had always lived in poverty seemed like miracles. When I was 10, my sister M immigrated to California with my two other sisters, leaving me with a sense of loss I had never quite experienced before. I remember driving her with some family to the airport and after she left and I went home with my grandparents, I broke down. Although my sister and I rarely expressed love/care for each other, it broke my heart to see her go. I felt like no matter where I went, I felt this sense of complete sadness and solitude. I stayed with my grandparents for the next three years and eventually managed to adapt and simply absorb this feeling of loss. I almost finished the 7th grade in Mexico before immigrating to the U.S.

At what age did you migrate to the Divided States?

Apatzingán, Michoacan is a mythic town, but also a very dangerous one. It's an agricultural powerhouse in the Central Pacific region of Mexico. Most people living there work picking up limes, mangoes, avocados, cucumbers, and more. It's very hot during the summer and has a very intense raining season. It's the city where the first version of the Mexican Constitution was drafted in 1814.[1] However, Apatzingán is also known for being the heart of various drug cartels and organized crime. The situation has been devastating for decades. Many orchard owners and business owners are extorted for money, and some decide it's safer to shut down and flee, leaving lots of people without work. People are kidnapped, disappeared, murdered, and more with authorities who are either colluded or lack the capacity to protect the people. While I lived there, every day the newspaper would pass in front of our house announcing through their speakers about newly found bodies in the center of town. Organized crime and the drug trade has plagued the city for many decades, leaving countless lives lost. Hearing of kidnappings and killings throughout the town became a normal thing. One time in the 7th grade, as I was in middle school, we were under an emergency drill after some drug traffickers had broken someone out of the prison located right behind our school. To me, all this seemed normal back then. I truthfully cannot say if I would be alive, had I not immigrated to California when I did. Over the years I have learned of childhood friends lost to either drugs or the endless violence in the city.

I was 13 years old when I immigrated to the U.S. I left my school, my friends, my home, but most importantly my abuelitos. At the time, I had no idea that as poor as we were and all the struggles we faced, everything I was leaving behind and how I would never be able to recover it. At the age of 13, I hastily made the decision upon being asked if I wanted to join my older sisters in California. To this day, I am not sure that it was the correct decision. I am not sure that there was truly a choice to begin with. Now in my thirties, I find regret in having left my grandparents, but I know that they would be happy to see me today and sometimes that is enough.

Now that you are older, why have you chosen to remain in the Divided States? Have you ever considered leaving the Divided States? Why or Why not?

I have been undocumented since I arrived in California in 2007. It was until 2013 that I qualified for DACA and gained the privilege to work legally and avoid the constant risk for deportation. Despite having these privileges for over ten years now, it has not been easy living with DACA. Remaining in this country comes at the cost of living in limbo, not knowing when the next time will be that politicians will decide to play with our lives as a pawn in their political games for power. Living under the previous administration was especially difficult due to their several attempts to terminate DACA and expel us out of the country. I remember being excited in 2020 when the current administration got into power and democrats regained the house and senate. I was excited that change would finally arrive, that there would be a path to citizenship for many immigrants in this country, but as previously demonstrated time and time again, politics are simply a race for power, often at the cost of human lives.

Certainly, there have been times when I have considered leaving. Especially when I lost my grandmother and then my grandfather without the ability to visit them to say goodbye. My main motivation to remain in California has been to pursue higher education and a better opportunity. I have also chosen to stay because I no longer have close family in Mexico. California is my home and my community is here.

What challenges did you face during the migration process?

At the age of thirteen, I traveled to Tijuana and was stranded there for weeks. I remember staying at a stranger's house and waiting for weeks to have the first attempt at crossing the border. The first attempt failed and I found myself alone at night in one of the most dangerous cities in Mexico. Having had to grow up and mature from an early age taught me to prepare, so I made sure to write a family member's phone number on a small piece of paper and put it in my shoe. I walked the streets for some time until I was able to find a store where I could make a call. A few hours later, I was picked up and back to waiting on for weeks to attempt to cross the border again. In the second attempt, I finally succeeded and arrived in the U.S. This experience makes me reflect on how dangerous the journey to make it here was. I could have been kidnapped/disappeared or worse as so many other immigrants have in their attempt to cross the border for a better life.

This is something that I wish more people in this country understood. Immigrants are not coming to this country to steal their jobs or take advantage of the system. People without documents do not have access to any form of federal aid, despite paying taxes every year. Some states like California have more resources for people without documents, but this is not the case for every state in the U.S. In addition, most undocumented immigrants work extremely hard in agriculture, construction, service industry, and other jobs that many U.S. citizens do not want to take. The reality is that people risk their lives and the lives of their family/children crossing the border because they simply do not have a choice. Most people do not want to leave their home and their loved ones while risking their lives coming into this country, but the situation in their home has gotten so desperate due to violence or lack of resources that immigrating is the only choice. It is noteworthy to mention that the U.S. has played a major role in creating the circumstances that force people to flee their home country. For example, U.S. policies have helped to perpetuate the violence in my hometown Apatzingán and Mexico overall. The majority of weapons found in Cartels' hands are manufactured in the U.S. and somehow, they end up in the hands of these violent groups. Whether it is through robbery, kidnapping, extortion, persecution or murder, normal people in Mexico end up paying the cost. The incessant violence in Mexico is of course very complex and does not inherit a single factor. I bring this up not to put all the blame on the U.S., but to bring light to the fact that U.S. policies undoubtedly play a major role in creating devastating circumstances in other countries that force people to migrate.

How did you adapt to a new culture, language, and way of life in the Divided States? What strategies did you use that helped you acculturate to the Divided States?

Adapting to the U.S. at the age of thirteen had a mirage of obstacles. I came to this country without being able to speak English and knowing very little about the culture. I was placed a year behind as I started in middle school. Through high school, I struggled academically due to not speaking the language. The high schools I attended were underfunded and did not make an effort to help lower Socioeconomic Status (SES) students go to college. I never considered going to college throughout high school because it wasn't something that anyone I knew had done. I barely graduated from high school with a low GPA and the bare minimum number of credits needed after attending summer school and night school. The fear of being chased by dogs from Mexico translated to the fear of being singled out by other kids and by gang members simply because I looked "Mexican." I remember a time in high school, I was running to catch the bus to go home, and accidently bumping into a kid who took it upon himself and his friends to mug and intimidate me for the rest of high school. I frankly couldn't even understand what their insults meant. College wasn't something high school counselors or teachers talked to us about. It simply seemed like a place we weren't meant to be.

I managed to adapt because of the resilience taught to me by my grandparents and by my well-developed instinct to survive from an early age. Despite the chaos of adapting to the social and academic environment of a new country, I tried to learn English as best as I could. With a few dollars I had, I purchased a small orange radio from the discount store, Ross. This being back in 2007-2012 and our poor upbringing, I didn't have access to computers or a cell phone. This small radio helped me listen to radio shows and music in English. I also had a yellow

English/Spanish dictionary, which I used to look up words I had heard in school or on the radio. It took time and effort, but I learned the language and learned to survive in a new, and not always friendly environment.

What aspects of your home country, if any, do you miss the most?

After living for 17 years in California, I sometimes do miss my home country. I especially miss our food, our traditions, and our rich culture. I miss my grandparent's home and the many memories of my childhood there. I miss the mole, albondigas, carne seca, caldo de pollo, chocomil de platano, los tamales, los sonidos, colores, y olores de la Navidad at my grandparents' home.

Can you describe a memorable experience or encounter you had when first arriving in the Divided States?

As soon as I arrived in the U.S., I started middle school in a low-income area. In order for us to enter the cafeteria to get our lunch, we had to leave our backpacks outside as a way to prevent kids from putting food into their backpacks. During my first day of school, as I went into the cafeteria to get my lunch, I had my backpack stolen. I recall coming out and restlessly looking for it all over. I remember feeling lost without being able to communicate to my teacher or anyone who could help me find my backpack. After that, I used my sister's old backpack which I ensured to take with me inside the cafeteria and instead show the people working at the cafeteria that I wasn't taking any food with me.

Another memorable experience was during my first summer in the U.S. After the end of the school year, I was to attend a summer school program called *Adelante (Forward)* with the rest of my classmates, but no one ever explained where it was and where I needed to take the bus to take me there. When the first day of summer school came, I assumed it was taking place at my middle school so I walked there and somehow was enlisted to attend despite the coordinators not finding my name. Well, the program taking place at my middle school was for troubled youth and somehow, I ended up attending that program instead of the one I was supposed to attend. Later when the Fall semester started, I found through my classmates that the Adelante coordinators were calling out my name without a response from me.

These experiences highlight some of the difficulties I encountered as an immigrant child in this country. They highlight the educational inequities that lower SES children must often experience in school. After reflecting on these experiences, it is almost incredible how I ended up going to college after all my earlier education experiences. It is no surprise that not many of us make it to college or even graduate from high school given all the barriers we must face.

How has immigration impacted your identity and sense of belonging to your immigrant community and the U.S?

Despite living in the U.S. for more than 17 years, I still have difficulty finding a sense of belonging. Even though I have been surrounded by diverse communities with progressive mindsets throughout my educational years, it still has been difficult to relate to most students because most students are not undocumented or DACAmented. There are things that documented people will simply never understand, like the feeling of not being able to travel to see your loved ones or the constant "you don't qualify for all these opportunities (work, internships, research, travel abroad) because you are not a permanent resident or citizen." And there have been multiple instances like this throughout my education despite being a DACA recipient. For example, when I applied to medical school, I wanted to apply to Universidad de Guadalajara School of Medicine, but as it turns out, only U.S. residents/citizens are eligible, despite the school being located in the country I was born in, Mexico. Additionally, many U.S. states do not even consider DACA recipients to their medical schools. As I worked on my list of medical schools to apply to, I found that more than half of the schools on my list did not accept people like me.

In the years 2018-2021, I lost both of my grandparents. The two beings who raised me and my sister when we most needed it. They lived in Mexico, and I was not able to travel to see them during their last moments or mourn them. This was because the previous administration revoked the ability of DACA recipients to travel abroad for any reason. The complexity of emotions I experienced as my grandparents passed away and I could do nothing to comfort them or see them one last time are hard to express. I felt powerless, hopeless, frustrated, angry, and a sense of injustice. This is something that only undocumented people can understand, the feeling of not being able to see your loved ones during their last moments, all for not leaving the life you have built with so much work and effort for the second time. Throughout college, I had friends who were able to travel abroad at any time and would come back with their vacation stories. I recall friends' tales of how they would go drink and party in Rosarito, Tijuana every chance they had while in college. This made me feel like I didn't belong. I felt angry and devastated seeing that I could not do such a basic thing like see my grandparents during their last moments, yet my classmates could travel abroad to party with so much ease. Of course, none of this was the fault of my friends, but it was still hard not to feel a sense of sadness and lack of belonging.

Additionally, since the last administration, immigrants have been scapegoated perhaps more than ever. It is much easier to put the blame on a vulnerable group of people and pretend that problems of this country like income inequality and racism are not deep-rooted and systemic. It is hard to feel a sense of belonging when your own humanity is taken away by terms like "aliens, criminals, illegal immigrants." To be clear, there is no such thing as an "illegal." Certainly, one can commit an illegal activity, break the law, but this does not make that person an illegal. For example, running a stop sign is an illegal activity, but does that make the person who perpetrates this action an "illegal"? If that was the case, then everyone would be an "illegal" given that most people break different laws at some point in their life. Clearly, these terms are used to strip people without documents of their humanity and make it easier to blame them for just about anything. This tactic has been used with several other minority groups in the U.S. through its history. Today, many U.S. politicians use DACA recipients and undocumented communities as pawns in their political campaigns, without considering the human lives behind it all. I have been a DACA recipient for nearly twelve years and I have stopped counting the times one party has vowed to pass immigration reform, while the other has vowed to deport us and has used us to stoke anger and fear in some Americans. Neither have occurred, but DACA continues to remain in great peril until today.

It has been difficult finding belonging in academia where most people I'm surrounded by have no idea of the many things I have had to go through to be in the same place. Even now in medical school, I have not encountered another DACA recipient in one of the most diverse medical schools in the country. Yet here I am, and although I feel alone at times, I know that this is not true. I have a community beside me, and I have the responsibility to empower future generations and help bring down the barriers that keep many of us from higher education and better opportunities.

Can you describe a memorable instance of discrimination or prejudice while migrating or after arriving to the Divided States? How did you deal with them?

When I was around 17-18 years old, I worked as a cook at a restaurant. One night after work at around 10pm, I headed to my car to drive home. At the time, I was undocumented and did not have a driver's license since the state of California did not give out licenses to undocumented immigrants. That night, a police officer followed my car from my work parking lot and pulled me over because my car did not have a front plate, although the rear plate was present. The officer asked for my license, insurance and registration. I provided my registration and insurance and stated that I did not have a license without revealing why. The police officer immediately assumed that I was undocumented without any proof. He started berating me demanding to know why I was working since I was *an illegal*, per his words. He then said to me with anger and hate in his voice, *I hope you know what you are doing is wrong.* Without authorization, he proceeded to search my car without reasonable cause, expecting to find drugs or something based on his behavior. He then impounded my car for a month, despite my plea to wait until my sister who did have a driver's license arrived to pick up the car. Recovering the car cost me about $2,000, at a time that I lived on my own, worked two jobs and went to school while barely making ends meet.

I felt angry at the prejudice and racism displayed by this police officer. I was not taking anyone's job because no U.S. citizen wanted to do this work, just like the work in the fields that many farmworkers do every day. Pursuing one's dreams in this country through hard work does not come at the cost of U.S. citizens, on the contrary, I contributed to this country paying my taxes every year without ever qualifying or receiving any federal assistance. During these younger years, I was angry and felt a deep distrust of police officers. Now, I am still cautious around police officers, but no longer fear them or feel anger towards them because I've decided to live with compassion and not hate. As a future doctor, it is my goal and desire to treat every patient with the same respect and compassion, no matter their background. I share this anecdote because I want to inspire readers to be informed of their rights, to not live in fear, and to live with love and not hate despite the racism many of us regularly encounter.

What successes or accomplishments have you achieved since migrating?

After immigrating at the age of thirteen, I started out in middle school and then transitioned to high school where I struggled due to the language barrier. I failed many classes as a freshman and sophomore in a high school with limited resources for the majorly Latinx student population. As a junior, I transferred to a high school with more resources where for the first time a teacher talked to me about what an essay was and where a teacher from Santa Rosa Junior College asked me what my educational plans were after high school. I worked to contribute to my household, attended night classes, summer school and anything in my power to recover the credits lost in my first two years. With much effort and perseverance, I learned English and graduated from high school, being the first one in my family to do so.

After high school, due to family financial difficulties, I moved out of my sister's home to live on my own and struggled to support myself while attending community college. At one point I found myself crashing on a friends' couch for weeks because I didn't have a place to live. My first two years of community college consisted of being placed on probation after failing the same Psychology and Math classes for three times in a row. I was taking more classes than I could handle given the hours I worked, but I didn't know, no one told me how to handle all of this. At the time, I rented a room in a family's home and worked at least two jobs simultaneously to support myself. In addition, along with two of my sisters, I was responsible for financially supporting our grandparents back in Mexico. There were times where I barely made rent, bills, and money for my grandparents with little money left to eat.

I worked at a carwash cleaning rims on my knees for hours, making minimum wage. I worked at various restaurants as a cook, busser, and dishwasher. I worked cleaning people's yards, carrying a heavy leaf blower that I could barely carry around. Working graveyard shifts at a restaurant caused me to fall asleep in my classes, but I had to work to survive. I felt ashamed after my math professor would wake me up during class, feeling like a failure no matter how much I tried to stay awake. At one point, I was in academic dismissal and nearly left college entirely. It took years of hard work and multiple failed attempts to figure it out, but I did it. I figured out how to save money, quit the carwash, and balance working less hours in my other jobs in order to sleep better and put more time into school.

I remember the first class I completed successfully and got an A. It was a high school level English class with a professor who for the first time saw my potential. She encouraged me to read the Hunger Games book and taught me to improve my writing. Around this time, I also started to build my community. I had a friend who was also struggling like myself, and who had attended the same high school. A counselor also saw something in me and to this day has remained an integral part of my journey in higher education. After five years, lots of dedication, work and grit, I graduated from Santa Rosa Junior College with my AA in Psychology and transferred to UC Davis to continue my education.

Prior to attending UC Davis, I applied and was accepted into the Stanford Summer Community College Premedical Program (SSCCPP). It was here that for the first time, I saw medical students and doctors who looked like me. One of the medical students, one member of SSCCPP leadership, and one doctor at Stanford became my mentors. They motivated me and opened my eyes to the fact that becoming a doctor was indeed possible and not a far-fetched dream. They helped me believe in myself and my ability to succeed in a field that has historically been reserved for people with lots of privilege.

After the SSCCPP program, I started my Bachelor's degree at UC Davis. Thanks to some savings I had and a bit more financial aid from the university, I was able to afford working less hours and concentrate on my studies. However, I still worked as a tutor and bus driver to afford my education. During this time, something that caught my attention and started to become more apparent as time went by is how underrepresented Latinx students are in Science, Technology, Engineering, and Mathematics (STEM). I noticed that the deeper I went into my science classes, the less people of color there were. Later on, when I took a Chicana/o Studies course, I noticed many Latinx students which helped me reflect on this issue. It is true that science is hard and requires a great deal of work and discipline, but that can't be the only reason why Latinx students choose different fields. There are indeed lots of barriers in STEM for students of color, including the lack of instructors who look like us, the extra resources needed to be able to succeed in STEM and many more. Today, I work on this by providing workshops and mentorship for younger underrepresented students back in my hometown Santa Rosa and students at UC Davis. I've developed great mentorship relationships with people along my path that have guided me and pushed me to go on. It is my intention to provide the same for others and that they do the same for future generations. I believe this is our best hope for creating change in medicine and in society overall.

After long hours of studying while working, I graduated with a B.S. in Psychobiology in 2020. During this time, I had the privilege to volunteer for Clinica Tepati, a community clinic in downtown Sacramento, to help provide free health care services to underserved communities in the Sacramento area. This experience taught me the importance of listening to patients with cultural humility and the importance of building trusting relationships with patients and the community. The patients I served resembled so much to my grandparents and the community in which I grew up and the very humane care and interactions cemented my desire to pursue a career in medicine. A curious fact about the name of Clinica Tepati is that the word Tepati was taken from the word *Tepatiliztli,* which means *to heal* in the Nahuatl language.[3] I find this very grounding as it represents the spirit of our ancestors in the care we provided to our patients.

After graduating, I worked as a health educator for a Federally Qualified Health Center (FQHC) in Sacramento where I provided health education in English and Spanish for patients to prevent and manage chronic conditions like diabetes and high blood pressure. The work I was able to carry out here was some of the most meaningful work I have done because I was able to work directly with underserved communities like my own.

In 2021, I went back to school and earned a Master's in Public Health (MPH) at UC Davis, all while working to pay my classes as a Teaching Assistant (TA) for a Chicana/o studies class as well as for the Biochemistry series. I remember a comment I received on my evaluation as a TA for Biochemistry which stated how the student was happy to see a TA in STEM who looked like her and spoke Spanish.

In 2022, after my MPH, I took the summer to study for the Medical College Admission Test (MCAT), the test needed to apply to medical school. As previously stated, there are many barriers to becoming a doctor, but this test is perhaps the biggest barrier of them all. It is a 230 question, 8-hour exam on topics like General Chemistry, Organic Chemistry, Biochemistry, Biology, Math, Physics, and more. It's a test that requires a great deal of time to study along with many other resources. Students have very different ways to study for this test, but not matter the case, preparing for this test is an extremely difficult challenge because of the difficulty of the test, but most importantly because of the resources required to prepare for it. I took 10 weeks to study full-time (about 80 hours per week). This came at a tremendous sacrifice, not only mental, physical, emotional, but also financial. I used all the savings I had and ran out of money towards the end of my studying. With a great deal of shame, I reached out to friends to help me afford my rent and groceries. Without their help, I would not have been able to complete taking the test. At the same time, I put together my medical school application and after 10 of the most intense weeks of my life, I took the MCAT and submitted my application to medical school. It is hard to describe what this time was like. I felt lonely, embarking on a journey that no one from my community had done so before. Just the fact that I had seen this summer all the way through the end was a huge accomplishment that I will never forget.

After I submitted my application, I waited for months to hear back from medical schools. During this time, I worked as a Clinical Research Coordinator for UC Davis. I worked to bring health education about Alzheimer's disease and brain health to underserved communities in the Sacramento area. I fostered amazing relationships with community members that are part of what fueled me during difficult times. After months of waiting to hear back from medical schools, my top choice UC Davis School of Medicine (UCDSOM) reached out and offered me an interview. I reached out to friends and mentors to help me prepare for the interview and my community showed up when I needed them most. Three weeks after interviewing, I received the news that I was accepted into UCDSOM. Reaching this point was the culmination of many years of hard work and sacrifice.

As a DACA recipient, just as when I was undocumented, I do not qualify for any form of federal assistance. All these years of school, I've had to work to support myself and afford my education with some help from the state of California as well. The higher I've climbed in terms of education, the fewer people I have seen who come from communities like mine. Now I am a first-year medical student at the University of California Davis School of Medicine and while there are a significant number of Latinx students (24%), we are still nowhere near where we should be in terms of representation, but we are making progress, nonetheless.

I have now successfully been in medical school for almost a year. To say that medical school is difficult is an understatement, but I find strength in knowing that my community needs doctors like me. I find strength in the resilience my grandparents taught me and I'm sure they would be happy to see me today. I find strength in my community. Despite how fast life passes by, and all the people and things I am forgetting while writing this, I reflect on the journey that has brought me here. I reflect on the younger version of myself who could have ended in a thousand different places, and despite all the barriers and disparities, here I am.

What advice would you give other immigrants who are going through the immigration process?

I would advise other immigrants to reach out for help. It often can be difficult to ask for help, especially for those of us who were raised with the mentality that we shouldn't inconvenience or bother others. Fear of deportation or encounters with law enforcement are real and can prevent many immigrants from asking for help, but frankly speaking, we need people, we need community. I would not be here without the support of my community.

I would also advise other immigrants to be patient and disciplined with their resources. In my workshops to high school and community college students, I often remind students to make wise decisions with their money. To not get into debt needlessly and instead to pursue higher education or a business with the proper guidance. After high school and throughout college, I remember wanting a new car, clothes, etc., but I remained disciplined to my goal of pursuing a higher education. I would frankly not be in medical school if I had not worked as hard as I did and if I hadn't saved money when I could. Success in achieving our dreams requires patience and discipline and I encourage other immigrants to be wise with their money in the pursuit of their dreams. As the saying goes, *Lo que vale la pena, toma tiempo (That which is worth a lot, takes time).*

I would also advise other immigrants to try to learn English and pursue an education. I acknowledge that it is not easy, especially when sometimes we are working hard to make ends meet, but I believe it is possible as I have seen it with my own eyes. It can start with finishing high school and going to your local community college and then transferring to a university or going straight to a university from high school if you have the opportunity. If you weren't able to get a high school diploma, go to your local community college and ask how you can earn your GED and pursue a higher education or a short career. I would advise to avoid getting into legal problems and to seek legal advice from reliable sources.

Lastly, I would advise other immigrants to seek resources for mental health and healthcare as there are options available with little or no cost, especially in California. Immigrants are resilient and know how to survive, but if we want to begin to thrive, we must make time to heal physically, mentally, and emotionally. The grit we possess is what fuels us every day, but it comes at the cost of many traumatic situations that many of us have had to encounter along our journey. In order for us to have better, healthier lives not only for us, but for our loved ones, we must work on healing our emotional trauma. It is not easy, but if we want to break the cycle of trauma and family dysfunction from generation to generation, we must be brave and finally begin to talk about these issues. No one is immune to depression, anxiety, substance use, domestic violence, and more, but it is up to us to start addressing these issues. As I tell some of the patients I work with, *la mente y el cuerpo son una misma y si queremos estar y sentirnos bien, tenemos que darle prioridad a nuestra salud mental también (the mind and body are one, and if we want to be and feel better, we must give priority to our mental health).*

Can you share a funny or heartwarming anecdote from your experiences as an immigrant?

An anecdote I would like to share is of a time when I was in high school. As I sat in the back of the classroom for my Spanish class, a person whom I had never met before entered the room. They shared with the class about college and asked if we planned on attending. Although, I can't recall the details of that day, I remember confronting this person and thinking *what does this person know about my life, what gives them the right to think they have an idea of who I am and what I have been through.* During my younger years, I was an angry teenager who felt alone and in pain. I felt abandoned by those I loved most and I used anger as my drug of choice. I didn't care about school and simply carried on with the motions. That day, I was angrier than usual because I think for the first time someone had looked at me and challenged me to remember who I really was and what I was capable of. I had forgotten myself and what I had been taught by my grandparents. I had forgotten that I mattered, that I was capable of achieving anything I set my mind to, and that I was not alone.

A few years later, this same person helped me as I stumbled my way through community college. Just when I was about to be dismissed after being placed on academic dismissal, I remembered someone had come to talk to us in high school about college. I looked for this person and this person was there. They guided me, supported me, and believed in me and to this day, this person has played a pivotal role in my journey. I share this anecdote to remind others that as long and dark as some days may seem, there are always angels in our path. People who care about us and genuinely want to see us succeed. There are good people in this world. We are not alone.

Have you had the opportunity to visit your home country since immigrating? How was that experience?; How did that experience make you grow?

I traveled to visit my grandparents after 10 years of not seeing them since I first immigrated to California. I traveled with Advance Parole for humanitarian reasons which I applied for months in advance. I was nervous and scared to go because I wasn't sure I would be able to come back given that Advance Parole does not guarantee reentry into the U.S. I was afraid I would not be able to come back to continue my education, but I took the leap of faith to see my grandparents. They were getting old, and I felt there would not be another chance to see them, so I took the risk.

It was early January of 2016 that I traveled alone to Guadalajara and then took a 6-hour bus to Apatzingán, Michoacan. I arrived in town in the evening and even after 10 years, I still recognized where I was. I took a taxi and gave the driver directions to my grandparent's home. On the way there, the taxi driver asked me where I was coming from and I responded from Guadalajara as to not reveal that I was coming from the U.S. The taxi driver immediately rejected this and stated that I was not from the area or Guadalajara and that I was coming from the U.S. I was shocked by his comments and later on reflected on the fact that my own *gente (people)* no longer recognized me or accepted me as one of their own. For the first time, I understood what many Chicanas/os experience, the feeling of not being *ni de aqui, ni de alla* (not from here, nor there), the feeling of no longer belonging to the country I was born in, the feeling of living in limbo in my country too.

Traveling those old, dirt roads and seeing the old houses brought me a feeling of nostalgia. I asked the driver to stop at the house next to my grandparents' where my aunt lives and got off the taxi. I was standing in the street where I grew up, where I played soccer, where I fell, where I laughed with friends. I knocked on my aunt's door and she came out. It took her a few moments to recognize me and then gave me a hug. I had not told anyone that I would be visiting. I was afraid that something would happen that would prevent this trip, so I decided to simply go without letting anyone know. I asked my aunt to come with me to my grandparent's home. We entered their home as my grandmother sat on her chair on the patio. She could not tell who I was from far away due to her worsening vision, but as I got close, I told her who I was. Initially, she did not recognize me and believed it to be a joke. She started screaming for my grandfather once she realized it was me. My grandfather came out and gave me a hug. Carefully, I looked at my grandparents. They looked much older than I remembered them, and I was overcome with a deep sadness. I felt that I had lost 10 years away from the two beings who raised me and cared for me and my sister when we most needed it. At that point I understood that this would likely be the last time we would be together and it broke me.

The house where I grew up was the same, still orange, surrounded by large mango trees, just a bit older and smaller than I remembered. In fact, everything seemed smaller and unreal. Initially, I had planned to stay there for at least a week, but I grew increasingly nervous the longer I was there. The few times I went to the center of town with my family, suspicious men stared at me up and down as if I was a foreigner. I became paranoid that I would be kidnapped by local organized crime and after only two days of being there, I purchased my ticket to return to the U.S. Although I dressed modestly and did my best not to bring attention to myself, people could tell that I was a visitor. Maybe my accent changed, the way I behaved, the way that I looked, I am not sure, but I was certainly made a stranger in my own country. Besides the paranoia, I worried that I would not be allowed back into the U.S. to the life that I had built for the second time. After just a couple of days, I came back to the U.S. My grandparents were sad that I left so quickly, but I like to think they were also happy that we got to see each other one more time. Some family mocked me for not having lasted more than a couple of days in Mexico and at the time it made me angry. Angry because what do they know about living as an undocumented immigrant in the U.S. and the many fears and anxiety we face. Over the years, I've learned that none of that matters. I am simply grateful that I took the risk and was reunited with them one last time. I hold on to these memories with love and gratitude.

What are your hopes and dreams for the future as an immigrant in the Divided States?

One of my dreams is to become a Family Medicine/Psychiatrist doctor in the near future and bring healthcare services to communities most in need. It is my goal to improve access to medical services and bring culturally competent care to all my future patients and continue to advocate for a healthcare system that is equitable. My commitment to serving the community stems from my own and my family's struggle with accessing healthcare services. It is my goal to be the doctor to my community that I wish my grandparents could have had.

I hope to encourage future generations to pursue their dreams and increase representation of people of color in medicine. It is my hope to inspire other DACA recipients and undocumented communities to never give up and continue fighting for a better opportunity for themselves and their families. It is my hope that undocumented immigrants and DACA recipients are given a path to citizenship and that those who have been unable to hug or kiss their mothers, their fathers, their children and friends are able to do so soon.

It is my goal to empower my nephews, nieces, sisters, and friends to believe in themselves and find the love and healing that they deserve. It is my hope to soon be able to travel to visit the resting place of my grandparents and mourn their loss, but most importantly to thank them and show them how far we have come.

It is my goal to instill in my community the importance of higher education and why it is essential for creating permanent change that dismantles inequality and oppression. There is a lot of hatred and injustice in the world, but there is also love, kindness and compassion. It is my dream that my community treat each other with acceptance, kindness and compassion and that it spreads to more communities and throughout our society. I hope that mental health continues to be destigmatized, and my community finds healing.

I dedicate this chapter to my grandparents, Sara y Enrique, because without them it would have never been written. I dedicate this chapter to my nephews and nieces and to every angel that has been in my path.

Itzel Lopez

"Every aspect of the American economy has profited from the contributions of immigrants." - President John F. Kennedy

(San Francisco 2004, a few months after arriving in the USA, that's my dad on the left)

The year 2004 was the year my life changed.

My name is Itzel, and I am an Immigrant. I was born in the beautiful city of Oaxaca de Juarez, Mexico in 1995, where I spent most of my childhood. I migrated to the United States of America when I was eight years old, about to turn nine. Life in Oaxaca was far beyond difficult. My family and I migrated to the States to find shelter, food, and a better life.

As I write about my experiences as an immigrant I want to acknowledge that everything I am saying is based on my memories as a child and teenager. Also, I would like to acknowledge that everything that I have lived through has only made me a better and stronger individual and I would not change a single thing. I am grateful for all of the sacrifices my parents have made for me and my siblings for us to have the life and privileges we have now. As I write this now, I know for a fact that the choices, decisions, and everything my parents did were only out of love and nothing less. They are my heroes and my inspiration. Thank you for reading my story.

My parents had many reasons to immigrate to the United States of America. The reason that drove them to make this predominant decision was poverty. My mom was a stay-at-home mom while my dad worked long hours as a carpenter. Money was never enough no matter how long my dad worked. I remember my dad coming home feeling helpless, worthless, and feeling that he wasn't able to do enough for us. Our house in Oaxaca needed a lot of repairs to make it a safe place to live in. To paint a picture, the four of us including my mom, my dad, my brother, and I had to share one room to sleep in. There was no living room, only the kitchen and the bedroom, everything else was out in the open. My dad decided to immigrate a year before he brought all of us with him. We lived without my dad for almost a year before he went back to Oaxaca to bring us to live in the United States with him. My dad didn't want to risk the possibility of the United States not being a safe place to live in, so he decided to migrate to the United States first to see what options we could have and what life in the States would be like. He soon realized that he could give us a much better life with opportunities, shelter, and food.

Walking through darkness

It was finally time to pack and get everything ready. My brother was ten and I was eight years old when it was time to walk through the desert to arrive at this fairytale-like place that I made up in my mind. I imagined this place to be and look identical to Disneyland. I watched many movies from Disney like Mickey Mouse, The Little Mermaid, many of the princess movies, and The Lion King. I also grew up watching Barney and Friends. Barney and Friends made The United States look like a perfect, happy, and friendly place. The little girl in me was enthusiastic about this trip.

I gave away all my toys and I still remember saying goodbye to my friends and my 3rd grade teacher. Since my dad had been in the U.S.A. for the past year, I had collected a lot of toys that he had sent me. A lot of the toys I had were very hard to get as a child in Mexico. I had a lot of Barbies, and Barbie houses, and in Mexico, those were very expensive toys. I remember my teacher's reaction when I told him I was going to the United States of America and letting him know that I would be back soon. I remember his face because he was serious and I didn't think he liked the idea. As a little girl, I was confused and sad that he wasn't as excited for me, but now that I am a grown-up, I understand why he had this reaction. There was no "coming back" to Mexico. Many of those who migrate here, don't go back. Yet, an eight-year-old could never know or even understand what that looked like. I also remember saying goodbye to my grandma. Again, my words were always "We are coming back". I was not sad because I had no doubt I would not be back. I loved Mexico, I loved my friends, and I loved my simple life eating beans, cheese, and tortilla tacos. I had no intentions or desires to have a different life than the one I had. Besides, my best friend Zucko lived there. Zucko was my three-year-old dog and there was no way on earth I would leave him behind, but since I couldn't bring him with me, my aunt took care of him until I would return.

We weren't allowed to bring anything on this trip, so I made sure that my dad shipped my favorite doll and a few other items to the US. Since we were walking for four days through the desert, we needed to have a light load of things. There were a few others who were walking with us. It almost felt like an adventure and my brother and I were very excited.

I recall my mom being nervous and scared throughout the plane ride. My dad was very protective over her and patient with all of us. Everyone was afraid, confused, and serious. Our first stop was Mexicali. This is the place where everyone who was crossing the border would get plenty of rest and food, and also prepare for the long excursion through the desert. Everyone in our group that was crossing the border had to know how to ride a bike. The goal was to drive the bikes throughout the desert until the tires would give up on us and explode. This was an exciting time for me because it was the time I learned how to ride a bike for the very first time. I learned to ride a bike in Mexicali as I was getting ready to cross the border. There have been many times when I wondered how I could share this memory with others. When one thinks about the first time they learn to ride a bike or swim, it's usually a fun and happy memory. As for me, this memory brings a lot of emotions.

Finally, we gathered our backpacks full of sardines, food, and water. Our goal was to leave as early as possible so we left at sunrise, the sun was very bright by that point. I still remember riding behind someone's back on the bicycle and the coldness of the morning hitting my face. One of my biggest memories of this particular moment was when our bicycle's tires finally tore apart and we had to leave the bikes behind and start walking.

I remember holding my mom's hand as I was walking and also playing with my brother, pushing each other and having a fun time. The scary moments were when we had to hide. Someone would yell "Escondanse" which means "hide". I would instantly fall to the ground and all you could hear was my big pink puffer jacket crashing into the dirt. My parents said I was so quick to hide, that they never had to worry that I wouldn't listen. To me, as a kid, this was all just a game. Now thinking about these memories, I cry and think to myself, how horrifying this was, and how sad it is that people have to go through this to escape poverty, unsafe areas due to criminal activity, and much more.

The nights in the desert were freezing. This is why I had a big puffer jacket, yet you could see my cheeks turning pink and my lips cracking because of the temperature drops. The moon at night was our lantern. The sky and everything else was very dark but the moonlight made it easy to walk through. We tried to sleep at night and not do a lot of walking mainly because we didn't want to make noise. We were told that at night "la migra" known as ICE was patrolling around the desert and could spot us quickly. I recall seeing patrols driving around with their flashlights or headlights. I could sense how terrified my parents were. I became aware that ICE were the enemies and we had to be quiet, on good behavior, and hiding at any time they showed up.

The last days in the desert were the scariest because we started to run out of supplies. First, we ran out of food. We started eating desert plants and sucking up their juice for water. This was mainly to try to stay as hydrated as possible before we finished the last drops of water we had. Eventually, everyone became dehydrated, tired, and hungry. We ran out of water in the middle of the day, the sun was bright and we could feel the heat in every part of our bodies. Luckily we were close to a water tank, just a few miles away. Finally, when we saw the water tank, everyone was so relieved and we took our last break before arriving in the United States.

A child learning to live in the United States of America

When I started school in the U.S. I became a different person. In Mexico, I was an outgoing and extroverted kid. As soon as I experienced life in the States I became shy, quiet, insecure, and withdrawn. Adjusting to the process was one of the most difficult things I've experienced in my life. I was teased many times for not knowing English. Learning English was not as difficult as making friends and connecting with others. I thought that my own culture would lend me a hand and help me out, but it turned out that most of the Hispanic/Latino classmates I had in my classes were too embarrassed to speak Spanish and translate for me. The culture shock was what disappointed me the most. In Oaxaca, I had many friends and all of my teachers were very nice, the culture was very different. I would constantly cry during the school day asking my teacher to take me home (Mexico). As I adjusted I kept hoping the day would come when my parents would say it was time to go back to Oaxaca.

When I thought things couldn't get any worse, things always did. I was in fourth grade a year after migrating to the U.S.A. when my family and I received a call that my dog

(Zucko) had passed away. My aunt described his death as if he had starved himself because of how sad and hurt he was because we abandoned him. Not long after that, we found out our other dog had run away. As a child, I couldn't get a break from things. I started to become more sad, and my sadness made me resent my parents without understanding at that age all the pain they were also facing.

As soon as I was finally adapting to my new elementary school the rent at my apartment complex was increasing, leaving my parents to make another difficult decision. We needed to move to a different apartment complex in the same town, but further away from my elementary school. I started 5th grade at a different school and I moved in the middle of the year for the second time. I didn't realize how much this can affect a child until I began my career and research. Children need consistency, this is how they build trust, security, and confidence. I did not like moving around, and change was scary and traumatizing to me even as I got older. The only thing I appreciated was getting transferred to a better school. The reason why I say it was better is because the kids were a lot nicer. Latinx girls and boys weren't afraid or embarrassed to speak Spanish. I also made a friend who had arrived from Guatemala not long ago. I didn't feel alone and it made me hopeful about things.

When I turned thirteen years old, I realized that I needed to get comfortable with the idea of living in the United States. I started to speak more English and made more friends. Many times, I got my anger and frustration out on my parents, and suddenly I started to misbehave at school too. I disliked many things about America, the idea of being alone, not having family close, and society's expectations. When my dog passed away I started to resent my parents for bringing me here. When my sister was born I found joy in little things again. Yet, talking to my grandma on the phone was only a reminder that I had to keep waiting until it was the right time to go back to Mexico. I think this is what frustrated me the most. As a kid, I always asked my parents "When are we going back to Mexico?". My parents would only have one answer, "when it's the right time, one more year".

Middle school years

Middle school years were challenging because I was no longer excluded from taking science or history classes. Most of my 4th, 5th, and 6th grade years were spent with a tutor or a resource teacher, so I missed out on a lot of elementary curriculum. This is why many subjects were always twice as hard for me including one of the most important subjects; math. I still needed to be placed in ELL classes in middle school, but I no longer needed extra support. For those who don't know what ELL classes are, they are designed for English language learners, students who just arrived in the country or speak another language at home. To be placed in regular English classes,

74

students must pass specific tests and be recommended by their teachers. I was one of the students who were recommended by my teachers but I still wasn't an English proficient student. Since I had the opportunity to be in other core classes I no longer felt excluded because I got to be with the "normal" teens. I was tired of being known as the girl who didn't speak English or had an accent. I finally participated in other activities such as sports and clubs. I developed a strong character and a big attitude. I started to hang out with the wrong crowd, trying to find support systems through others who also didn't know where they were in life.

I connected with a few teachers, but only one stood out to me the most, and that was my Physical Education teacher. Mrs. Kraus saw something in me that other teachers didn't at that time. She saw my resilience, optimism, and intelligence. Thanks to her I was able to be in the Track and Field team and represent my middle school at Track Meets. I was good at jumping hurdles regardless of my height. Mrs. Krause was tough on me because she knew I was smart enough and I would never give up easily. In many of the Track Meets, I won 2nd and 3rd place. This is where I slowly started to build strong self-esteem.

Adapting to life in America

Middle school years went by very fast. I learned a lot by making mistakes, misbehaving, following the wrong crowd, and more. Once I got into High-school I felt like a new girl, positive and confident. I started to feel comfortable speaking English and making friends. I liked living in California and I no longer wanted to go back to Mexico. By the age of sixteen, I had already lost members of my family and pets that were in Mexico. I adapted to living in the States by reading, playing my guitar, poetry, and doing crafts. I spent most of my evenings running outdoors or babysitting my sister. The apartment complex I lived in felt like home.

I adapted too well to the culture in America. I started to meet people with similar interests and also found things I enjoyed. I got used to listening to everything in English. Since my friends didn't like to speak Spanish, I also didn't speak Spanish and I would listen to English music like Ed Sheeran, Taylor Swift, and other artists that were popular at that time. I was always very proud of being Mexican but socializing and being around the white culture made me a different person. I started to date people that weren't Mexican. Being white was always seen as a good and superior thing and that's what I grew up learning. I remember having a classmate who was an exchange student from Germany and everyone was amazed by him, even teachers. This wasn't something new to me because even Latinos give more attention to white people. I remember in Oaxaca when we had tourists that were white, people would praise them and invite them into their homes. As a teenager, I felt this was normal and I did the same. I would respect them more especially because most of my teachers were white. I didn't have any Latinx teachers to look up to and this indeed changed my high-school experience. As I am sharing this experience, I want to make clear that I enjoyed having good role models that were not from my race or ethnicity. I don't recall experiencing any discrimination or racism by educators. However, I would have appreciated having had more teachers and educators who were similar to me, someone I could identify with as I was navigating through this big change in my life.

Identity as an immigrant

As I was growing up, I would hear negative things about being an immigrant. I wanted to hide who I was and I disliked talking about my identity and how I got to this country. I disliked the question "Were you born here?". I was ashamed of being known as an immigrant and that my friends knew about it. I disliked topics about traveling and the typical conversations about vacations to Mexico that a lot of my classmates took over winter break. I remember feeling upset, isolated, and alone. From my understanding, not being born in the United States meant that you couldn't travel back to your own country. When I was a kid, I first thought that we couldn't go back to Mexico because I needed to be with my family and stay together. As a teenager, I started to understand the actual meaning of why we couldn't go back yet, and that's because we were all waiting to get "papeles" (become legal and get documented).

Another part of learning English and understanding life in America was that I was not allowed to speak Spanish. By the time I started speaking English, I hardly spoke Spanish anywhere other than at home. The reason for this was mainly because no one liked to speak Spanish at school. Even though most of my friends were Latinx, we spoke English and most of them always wanted to listen to English music and follow trends that were away from our own culture. Part of fitting in and shaping our identity was to not be recognized as an immigrant.

In 2014, I applied to DACA (Deferred Action for Childhood Arrivals). For those who might not know or begin to understand, having DACA means that we are worthy of working in the United States, but we are not worthy of being documented. At least, that's how I've felt ever since I filed for DACA. I am grateful for DACA because I can work legally and drive legally, however, it is also a reminder that every two years I have to think about my identity as an undocumented person in the United States. I've had to file taxes on time, drive safely, not commit any traffic violations, be on a perfect record, and constantly worry about being a perfect "citizen" without being an actual citizen. I have worked countless hours, sometimes more than 40 hours a week. I have paid college and University tuition and helped contribute to my parents. I have a bachelor's degree in Spanish and Sociology and a master's Degree in School Counseling. However, every year that I have to file for DACA I feel less of a human. Whenever I hear news about DACA coming to an end or actual U.S. citizens committing crimes or wasting their lives each day, a rush of heat flows through my veins thinking, how is that justice? I often think, where do I fit in? I am Mexican but I can not travel there, and I feel like the United States is my home but I'm seen as an "Illegal Alien" here. I know my parents did the best they could, I am thankful for every single thing they've done for me. I just wish DACA recipients wouldn't feel

the way I do because if there is something we have in common, it's the pain that we relieve every two years when we file for DACA.

(Photo: My dad, me, and my mom days before receiving my master's degree. May 2023)

Adulthood

As I've looked through my life as a kid and teenager who grew up trying to figure out what was going on in my life and what my status was here in America, I started to become grateful for the sacrifices my parents made for me and my siblings. It took a very long time to come to terms with myself and let go of all the anger, frustration, and resentment I had built towards them through the years. It also meant that I needed to take care of myself. I started to go to therapy when I was twenty-four years old. I needed to understand that to help others I needed to not only understand myself but also help myself first. I still have the fears that I've had as a kid, especially others knowing I am undocumented. People see you negatively when they know you are undocumented. People feel pity, feel sorry and they also treat you differently. I have spent a huge part of my life accepting that being undocumented doesn't make you less of a person, but society has shaped many of us to think this way.

As an adult, I have battled with feelings of sadness and frustration not knowing when DACA can come to an end. I wish there were more spaces for undocumented students and professionals where we can speak about our feelings and everything we have to face. I know some colleges and Universities that provide this type of support, but I'd like to see it in other settings too.

Advice from an immigrant to others

I wish I had someone who had walked me through what it was like to transition from one country to another. Someone that could have helped me understand what I was going through. When I was doing my internship to become a school counselor. I had the opportunity to create a safe space for newcomers. This space focused on emotional, academic, and social skills as students transitioned into life in the U.S.A. I ran this group in Spanish, providing students with resources on how to take care of themselves as this was a critical time in their lives. To this day, now that I am a school counselor at a middle school, I try to provide a safe place for newcomers.

It is shocking how little resources we have for students coming from different countries.

One of my biggest advice to all newcomers or anyone who's been in the States but doesn't know where they fit in is to never forget your culture. It is okay to speak your language and no one should tell you otherwise. It is okay to be angry, frustrated, and have a mix of feelings. The most important thing is to remind yourself where you came from, where you want to get to, and what you need to do to get where you want to be. This can mean, if you are a teenager, always make school a priority. Our education is the strongest power we can ever have, even if we are undocumented.

Traveling back to Mexico after 19 years

After receiving my master's degree in school counseling, I had an opportunity to travel back to Mexico. I followed the necessary steps which included applying to Advance Parole. Advance parole is only granted to DACA recipients who are in good standing, and you are only accepted for advance parole if you meet three of their criteria. These are; traveling for educational purposes, work, or an emergency. Even though this was a very unique and exciting opportunity, I was sad that I wasn't able to do this with my family. Having this permission to leave the country did not guarantee that I was allowed to be back in. The day I left I cried as the plane departed. I cried mainly because I wasn't sure if that was the last time I would see my family. I was afraid of leaving everyone behind and I forgot about the excitement of seeing my birth country. I call the United States my home because that's what I know the most. I didn't know what Mexico was like for the past nineteen years. Therefore, seeing the lights of the city as the plane departed was a very sad and confusing experience.

Everything about Mexico seemed the same as what I remember. The food, the people, and everything about it. I unfortunately was not able to travel to my birth city Oaxaca. The permission I got was only to visit Jalisco. I was still very excited and everything about the trip was beyond amazing. I was in Mexico for about five days. As soon as it was time to board the plane and head back to California I was filled with a lot of emotions and not knowing what would happen. There came memories of when I first came to the United States and everything I have gone through with my family.

Finally, I arrived at the Oakland International Airport and my parents and my sister were waiting for me. There was a feeling of safety that came to me when I hugged my parents, and also the thought of how many family members wait to see their families but never get the opportunity.

The end of this chapter

As I conclude this chapter of my life, I am grateful to have told a small version of my story. This was just a summary of things because there are many parts of my life that I did not mention. The life of an immigrant is challenging, hurtful, frustrating, and traumatizing. I am grateful for the life I was given and I am a proud DACA recipient. My only wish is to inspire those who have taken the time to read my story. I'd like to dedicate this to both of my grandmas who rest in peace, to my parents, my siblings, and all the undocumented students who struggle to find their own identities.

Thank you.

Carlos Madrigal Lara

My name is Carlos Madrigal Lara and I was born in a small rancho (farm) in Puruandiro, Michoacán, Mexico. I was born on July 25, 1998 and shortly after, my family and I came to the United States in March of 2002.

Prior to bringing his family over, my dad had been coming to the United States to work since he was 18 years old. As I am writing this, my dad is 51 years old which means that he has been working physically intense jobs for about 33 years with no proper rest. His mind and body are tired, and you can tell simply by looking at him.

Before living in the U.S. permanently, my dad was traveling back and forth between Mexico and the U.S. working to provide for his family. My dad had been going between Mexico and the U.S. for about 8 years before he decided, alongside my mom, to bring us all over to the U.S. During the time that my dad was traveling between the two countries, my two sisters and I were born.

I have a sister who was born five years before me, Griselda but we call her Gris, another sister who was born two years after me, Brenda, and a younger brother born in the U.S. nine years after me, Andres. While my brother was born in the U.S., my sisters and I were born in Mexico in the same rancho my dad grew up in.

In March of 2002, my older sister was eight, I was three, and my younger sister was 1 year old. My older sister has vague memories of Mexico while Brenda's and I's memories are all here in the U.S. Initially, my parents had decided that they would come to the U.S. for a couple of years and eventually return back to their home in Mexico.

My parents had the idea that they would both work for a while and save money in order to live more comfortably with their family in Mexico. In their heads, they would return to the country they were raised in and see their families once again in a newly built home that they would construct from their hard-earned money in the U.S.

Now we have been living in the U.S. for about 22 years without having been able to visit Mexico, since we left.

(This is me when I still lived in Mexico, I was about two years old)

In the time that I spent in Mexico, I was raised mostly by my mom and my dad's mom, my grandmother whom we all call mama Maria. My mom tells me that as a kid, I loved spending time with her and often followed my grandma as she went to church or spent time with her friends. Mama Maria is what my siblings and cousins call her as she was like a mother to us. I have a lot of love for mama Maria and even though I don't have any memories of her, I know that she had a lot of love for me too. My parents told me a story that I will never forget, which demonstrates how much love I had for her as a kid. On the day that we left our home in Mexico, we stopped to eat tacos prior to crossing the border. My parents were confused because they had ordered two tacos for me, but I had only eaten one. When they asked me why I hadn't eaten the other taco, I told them that I was saving it for mama Maria. I didn't know that I wouldn't ever have the opportunity to ever give her that taco that I was saving for her.

After a couple of years living in the U.S., my parents realized that their initial goal of returning to Mexico wouldn't be so easy. At the same time, staying here is also not easy but at least their children are living better lives than they did as children. Here, in the U.S., my siblings and I have had the privilege of going to school for a higher education to achieve more than what my parents had the opportunity to. This is what is most important to my parents. After realizing that we would probably stay in the U.S. for longer than expected, my parents urged us to continue going to school after high school. I knew how much my parents suffered from their jobs as I saw them coming home extremely exhausted from work six days a week. They were doing everything in their power for us to have better lives here in this country. I knew I had to pursue a career by continuing school after high school. Seeing their children graduating from college and receiving jobs that are not as physically intense as the ones they have to work is what gives them the most joy and pride.

Nonetheless, coming to the U.S. is an extremely risky process, but it is a choice made due to the circumstances in which one lives. For example, my dad as a man has always had to work physically intense jobs from a young age simply to survive in Mexico. As a child, his dad would take him and his siblings out into the mountains before sunrise to work the fields. These fields they took care of provided for their families in Mexico. Many times, they left without any breakfast or any sort of lunch to eat while out in the mountains. They would end up coming home late at night and sometimes they would have some food for dinner. They wouldn't eat much because there wasn't any food to eat. The next morning the children had to wake up once again to work. This was just how life had to be for my dad and his family growing up. As for my mom, she had to take care of all her siblings as a child because she is the eldest girl. As a result, she had to be a mom from a very young age in order to allow her mom to take care of house duties. In Mexico, this is not unusual because women are often tasked with the responsibility of being caretakers from a young age, though it is extremely unfair. For both my parents, their childhood was taken from them because of the circumstances they were born into.

The process of entering the U.S. is unpredictable and expensive. For my parents, they had to cross the border on foot without their children and with the help of experienced people. My parents had to enter the U.S. first to guarantee that we wouldn't be alone in the U.S. Thankfully, they were successful on their first try and once they were in a safe place, they sent for their children. My sisters and I entered with the help of a married couple entering the U.S. "legally" because during this time, they didn't ask for our documentation. We entered at night, so my sisters and I were asleep while crossing the border. To make sure that we wouldn't wake up we were also given sleeping medicine to avoid risking anything. Once we had crossed the border we met up with our parents. This process was an investment my parents had to make. Financially, they had to borrow money from close friends to make these payments, which actually took years for them to pay back. Nonetheless, it was very much worth it for everyone involved.

Growing up in the U.S. has been difficult for many reasons. For my older sister who was eight when she got here, it was a lot more difficult to learn a new language because she was a bit older. Nonetheless, by the time she was out of high school, she was writing, reading, and speaking a lot more comfortably than my younger sister and I. For my younger sister and myself, the language was less challenging because we were so young. We don't even remember thinking about learning English. For us, it was all of a sudden and we had to help our parents with translating because we knew English. Still, according to state standards, I wasn't able to get out of language development classes until I was in 7th grade. For my parents and others, I knew English but at school, I was still struggling because I was being told I didn't know the language enough. At home all we spoke was Spanish and at school all we spoke was English. Language is a big part of one's identity, so we had different identities at school and at home. This was not something that I would realize until I became older.

Since I was a child, I remember our parents told my siblings and me not to tell anyone that we weren't born here. We had to be secretive to not give out our identities because it could have meant that we'd be sent back to Mexico. At this age, Mexico was a country that I knew nothing about besides that my family and I were born there and that we didn't want to be sent back. As a result of my parents sternly telling us this, I reacted by closing myself off from other people. I didn't want anyone to know who I was. I learned to be quiet and keep to myself. Teachers thought that I didn't want to talk because I was shy, but in reality I was terrified. I only shared out when I felt it was absolutely necessary or when I was forced to by my teachers. With my friends I was the same way; I didn't talk much with them during school. At home, with my neighborhood friends, I was the opposite. I loved being outside playing soccer and hanging out with them. Similarly to my language identity, I was two different people.

(I was about 9 in this picture, receiving an award at my
elementary school)

Figuring out my identity was one of the biggest struggles
I had as a child. This was because I knew I wasn't born in this
country, but I also knew that if I was in the country that I was
born in, I wouldn't fit in. I didn't know where I fit in because I
didn't have someone similar to me to relate with. This experience

is unique to first generation students. As time went by, I started to feel more comfortable with myself. Since we were so poor, I also had to deal with what we had and what we did not. I knew this so I knew not to complain, but this also meant that I never got the chance to explore who I was until I was a lot older. As a child I loved playing soccer and that was about it; in return this was the majority of my identity. During school, soccer was my whole identity, all I knew was soccer. Not having the opportunity to discover my identity as a child became an issue as I got older. As my environment changed after high school, I started to feel more and more uncomfortable because I was experiencing new things, and I didn't know how to respond.

A clear example of this was when I started to play soccer for my junior college. As a child, I had the privilege of playing club soccer for about ten years, since I was about eight years old. I had been playing with the same people the whole time, so we all developed to play comfortably with each other. Nonetheless, my club experience had to end at some point, and I wasn't sure if I wanted to continue playing soccer now that I was in college. My cousin, who I had grown up with and played soccer with since I was young, persuaded me to try it out. I remember the first time I went to practice, I struggled to get out of the car because I was so anxious, so we were late to practice. I continued to go to practice but it became a very anxious experience and even after completing the process of tryouts, I decided not to play. I was playing soccer at a good level during practice and the coach appreciated my playing style a lot, but I could not continue with the process. I felt horrible because this was the biggest part of my identity as a child, and I really did want to play soccer at the college level, but my anxiety was stronger. I told the coach that I couldn't play because I was struggling with anxiety and as a result he helped me receive the help I needed.

As a college student, I was able to receive therapy as part of my tuition, but I had never gone to seek help. The soccer coach got me in contact with someone from their offices to assess what I was struggling with. As a result, I was able to receive weekly therapy sessions for two semesters. The first semester was especially difficult as I was really struggling mentally and as a result, I failed two classes that semester. The second semester of receiving therapy was a lot better as I managed to pass all my classes with A's. I remember after every therapy session feeling extremely exhausted because each session was very intense. Regardless, I felt like I was making progress with myself, so I knew that if I wanted to get better, I had to be completely honest with my therapist and myself. I continued being honest and I continued to make a lot of progress. I began feeling more comfortable with myself and with seeking help when I needed it. I also began acknowledging when I was struggling mentally, and this was especially useful given the circumstances in which I was raised.

As a man, I was taught to only portray "masculine" emotions. I was only allowed to show emotions such as anger, and if I showed "feminine" emotions, I would be teased and scolded by the men surrounding me. This was difficult to adapt to because as a kid, I would tend to cry a lot and as a result, I learned that it wasn't okay to cry. As I got older, I eventually adapted and started to be more stoic. Seeking help even when I wasn't okay mentally wasn't something that I felt comfortable doing; I didn't grow up learning to seek help when I needed it. Being an immigrant, therapy was also not much of an option because services like these were a luxury that we couldn't afford financially. As a matter of fact, seeking any type of medical help was a luxury we couldn't afford given that we didn't have any type of insurance. There was a time in my freshman year of high school where I was accidentally hit in my eyebrow with a hockey stick in P.E. class. My eyebrow was slit open, and I was bleeding a lot, but I couldn't feel any pain because of the adrenaline. Going to the emergency room was what any normal person would've done, but we didn't have that luxury. Instead, I had to wait for the earliest appointment at my local clinic to be treated. By the time I was treated my head had been hurting severely, but I didn't hold it against my parents. I understood it was just what we had to do.

Growing up I always knew that this is how we had to live, so it was never something that I resented my parents for. I always understood that they were doing everything possible for my siblings and I to live decently. On the contrary, instances like these made me feel anger towards the system for being set up against people like me. Not only do we experience racism from people, but we also get to experience systematic racism. Experiencing racism growing up while knowing there wasn't much I could've done was depleting and exhausting. Knowing that my parents also experienced similar situations more frequently — and yet they still managed to do so much for my siblings and me — meant that I simply didn't have an excuse not to pursue their only desire for us. Their only request for us was to continue education after high school. Since I was in middle school, I knew that I would continue school into higher education. At the time I didn't know anything about college, but I did know that I was going to receive a bachelor's degree.

I had no other option, so after high school I attended my local junior college to follow in the footsteps of my sister. Gris also attended college, so by the time it was my turn, I had my sister to help me out with the process. I knew that I would be going to junior college so in high school, I didn't ever give it my best try. I did the bare minimum to get by and earned decent grades. I also did this because I was constantly mentally tired; I had not had the best childhood given the circumstances in which I had to live in. I learned to always be alert and aware of my surroundings. I always had to be paying attention and analyzing everything because I didn't know what might happen next. I always had to make sure nobody knew who I was. It may have seemed like I was doing the bare minimum but given the circumstances, I was doing the best that I could give. As a result,

I would end up staying at my junior college for three and a half years instead of the expected two. During this time, I received the mental help I needed with just a semester left on my own before transferring to a four-year college. Eventually I would end up receiving my bachelor's degree and continued for another year to receive my teaching credential.

Earlier I mentioned that in middle school I always knew that I was going to college even though I didn't know much about college. Well, when I was 15, I became eligible for DACA and so I had to apply. In the application, there is a question asking about future plans. This is a question because a requirement for DACA applicants is that we are either in school or work a fulltime job. I decided, alongside Gris, that I wanted to study mathematics in college. I decided this because it was my best subject and because I enjoyed math. I had no idea what I wanted to do with math, but at the age of 15 I had to make such a huge decision that I felt obliged to fulfill because of DACA. During my time in high school, my sister was working on her Bachelor's Degree in Chicanx and Latinx studies. My sister was and continues to be extremely passionate about this subject, but at that age I honestly was not. My sister would often talk to me about what she was learning but I was not very interested in what she had to say. By the time that I graduated high school, everything my sister would talk to me about made me realize what I wanted to do with math. Gris was learning a lot about systematic racism and how it was affecting us and people like us.

She taught me that the percentage of People of Color receiving a bachelor's degree or higher was very low compared to white people. This wasn't because People of Color aren't able to complete a higher education, it is because we don't receive the same opportunities as white people. We have not been able to see ourselves in higher education which makes it feel like we don't belong in higher education. This is not true whatsoever and as I continued to see my sister succeed in college in an area that she was clearly passionate about, I realized that I as well had to inspire students of color to pursue higher education. By the time I started college, I knew that I wanted to study mathematics to become a secondary education math teacher. By doing this, I would become a person that students of color could look up to and hopefully see themselves in. Students of color would realize that they belong in positions of "authority" and in fields like STEM.

After graduating high school, my goal would be to become a person who can inspire People of Color to pursue careers in STEM by allowing them to realize that if I was able to do it, they could too. Growing up in this educational system, I had about three teachers of color and that was about it through my whole K-12 education. I became aware that this was just unacceptable, and I felt like I had the privilege to become a teacher of color, so I decided to pursue this career. I would go on to study mathematics at my local junior college. Instantly, I learnt that I could not do the same thing I was doing in K-12. I had to

truly dedicate myself to my education and this was very difficult.
To begin with, the first couple of years I took the bus to college
and what was an hour ride on the bus, was a car ride that would
only take about 15 minutes. This would make my days so much
longer, but the ride was also relaxing sometimes.

There was a semester when I had to take the bus before 6 a.m. to
school and wouldn't get home until 9 p.m. I didn't realize this at
first because I just had to take the bus, I didn't have an option,
but this was a testament to my determination to receive my
bachelor's degree and just one of the barriers in the way of
earning my degrees.

Learning math at the junior college level was difficult as
it was a lot of individual work. I felt that throughout my time
here I didn't talk to many people. This was also because I was
very much alert about meeting new people and being careful that
they wouldn't know who I truly was. In the math department,
everything was individual work, where the professor would
project their notes and we'd have to follow along taking notes.
Everything about this junior college felt very difficult and it was
because I felt like I was all alone. If I needed help with anything,
I had to seek that help by talking to professors. Still, all my
professors were white men and so I was never truly comfortable
seeking help. My professors would say anything about how we
are more than welcome to talk to them during office hours, but I
still didn't feel comfortable. Nonetheless, I did seek help from a
couple of professors a couple of times, and I was starting to

speak up for myself a lot more than I did when I was in high school.

After three and a half years at the junior college, I would finally be transferring to a four-year university and my very first class that I took was a complete shock. For the first time, I had a female professor in an upper division math class. She began the first day of class by acknowledging her privilege of being white. Hearing that on the first day of class was one of the best feelings that I have ever felt because I had finally felt like I was noticed. Even though she was white, she was acknowledging the fact that I existed and that I could succeed in upper division math courses. Her teaching philosophy was also very different from anything that I had

ever experienced. In this class, she mentioned that she would never lecture and sure enough she never gave a single lecture. Instead, we would always work in groups where we learned to persevere and struggle together. This was sending me the message that I did not have to be alone to struggle; I could allow myself to open up to others to help me be successful. My professor would be monitoring the groups to make sure that we were struggling and guided us. Quite frankly, I was surprised at first, but her structure was something that I truly appreciated and looked up to.

My time at the university was very different than at the junior college so I enjoyed the university a lot more. I had more diversity with my professors and even had a teacher who was Polish. Here, a lot of my classes were about group work, and I was able to connect with peers because we were on similar paths. By this point, a small group of us knew each other because we had many similar classes, and we were on the path to becoming math teachers. I became very good friends with two Latina peers who wanted to become high school math teachers. I always had my eyes set on middle school, but still we connected and related with each other. We met in our last year of undergrad and became very good friends outside of school. These relationships were and continue to be very important to me because they have helped me grow as a person a lot and because we would go on to graduate from college together. Our last year of undergrad was very stressful but knowing that we were all going through it together felt very comforting. This was a new feeling that I was experiencing, and I felt very privileged to not be alone.

After receiving my Bachelor's Degree in Mathematics with a focus in Secondary Education, I continued the credential program at the same university where I got to meet more great professors who truly dedicated themselves to our success. My dad didn't understand why I couldn't just teach after receiving my bachelor's degree so he would constantly nag me about when I would be done. After explaining the process to him a total of what felt like 100 times, he finally understood that after receiving my teaching credential I could finally work and receive a full salary. Nonetheless, I began a year-long credential program where I was placed in a middle school. For the program, we were placed at a site where we would "work," without pay, in the mornings and in the afternoons, we would go to our own classes. This year was extremely stressful. I feel like I aged at least three years, but it was so rewarding in many different aspects.

To begin with, I was able to be fully funded and I didn't have to worry about money this whole year. Before entering the program, we are recommended not to work because the workload is a lot. It is like we are working full time and going to school full time. During the first semester we had a lot of class assignments, but we only had to be at our sites for a total of 100 hours to observe our mentors. I had joined a residency program that gave me monthly stipends, so I had to be at my site three days a week which was roughly three times more than other candidates in the credential program. For the second semester, we had to take over two class periods as teachers and continue to assist our mentors in two other class periods. Since I was in the residency program, I was at my site every day from the beginning to the end of school. After going to "work" I was going to my own classes about two to three times a week. On top of this, in the second semester we had to complete our edTPA which is a national, subject-specific portfolio-based assessment. The credential program was a lot of work, but I felt prepared and again, I just had to do it.

Even though learning English wasn't necessarily difficult growing up, it is not my first language and I do not speak English at home. Growing up, we only spoke Spanish at home so assessments such as edTPA are just hurdles preventing People of Color from reaching higher positions. EdTPA is an assessment where realistically, you will pass based on how well you can write. It is meant as an assessment to see if you are ready to become a teacher, but as an immigrant we are at a disadvantage because it is not a fair assessment for us. EdTPA is also very difficult to pass on the first time in general, so I knew that I was going to have to put more effort to pass. This is exactly what I did, and I gave myself plenty of time to do everything because I really wanted to pass on the first time. I did exactly that, I passed edTPA on my first attempt and this was a very proud moment for me. Only two of the seven math candidates passed on the first attempt and although that was unfortunate for them, I knew that my hard work was starting to pay off. As a result, I was able to complete the teaching credential program.

During the credential program I was also able to secure a job at my desired middle school location. My idea was always to return to the middle school I had attended and, quite frankly, this was to heal my younger self. Since I had not had the best childhood, I felt like a lot of it originated here so I always knew I had to go back to teach there. An old teacher from high school is now an administrator in the district and we had maintained contact because she had given me a job after high school as a tutor. She notified me that a position had opened up, but at the time I was extremely busy with edTPA and so I told her that I wouldn't be able to submit my application for another month. She said that it was okay, so after submitting edTPA, I began to work on the application. Roughly a month after, I submitted the application, and I received a phone call that they wanted to interview me. I began to panic. I was definitely scared. However, that same morning I went in for the interview, I got the news that I had passed edTPA, which gave me a big confidence boost. I was still nervous but as I went into the office, all of my anxiety went away. I knew what I was doing and that I belonged there.

I ended up receiving the job and I was extremely happy and grateful. The process had gone by so quickly; I submitted the application on a Monday and by Friday I received the call that they wanted to give me the position. Now that I have a job as a teacher – having worked hard, earning a bachelor's degree and a teaching credential – I do not see myself returning to Mexico other than for a limited time. I would love to return one day to the country that I was born in, but I definitely don't see myself living there for good. I will return at some point, but considering that I am a recipient of DACA, I cannot do that currently. Since I was a child, I knew that if I left this country there was almost no possibility that I could return. I could only see myself in this country, so I would never think about leaving this country. On the contrary, if I was thinking about leaving this country it would only be during times that I was feeling negative emotions. Still the only option was to simply stay put. I had never dreamt of traveling anywhere outside of the U.S. until more recent times when advance parole became an option. Since then, I have thought of leaving this country for a limited time to visit my only grandparent that I have left.

A hope of mine is to be able to visit my grandpa since I was not able to visit my other grandparents before their passing. This has been something that is very difficult as an immigrant because the passing of someone is already filled with emotions that are difficult to process. Now imagine that your parents have passed away in a different country than the one you reside in, and you can't visit them one last time. This is something I think about often because this is exactly what happened to my parents. For my dad, both of his parents passed away in Mexico and for my mom, her mom passed away in Mexico, too. They did not have the option to visit them one last time because they wouldn't be able to come back into the U.S. I cannot even try to imagine how they felt when this happened to them. Unfortunately, this is the weight we must carry in order to simply live more comfortably. It is tragic for my parents and all our families, but we just have to continue to live like this.

As I continue in my first year of teaching, I am excited for the future to continue growing as a person and an educator. I hope to continue to inspire students of color to pursue careers in STEM but also just to pursue higher education. I hope for students to see that a person with similar circumstances to them is in this position, that they have someone to look up to. I hope that my students know that when they are struggling with anything in their life, they can feel comfortable coming to me to explain their situation and seek help. This will not be easy and it will be a heavy task to fulfill but if I am able to help one student, I will be happy and know I have made a difference. I hope that soon my parents will be able to work less so that they can relax their minds and bodies because they deserve to rest. As much as they need to continue working their physically intense jobs, they also need to rest. Sometimes I think they don't realize this because they have been working so hard for so long. I hope to continue to make my parents and everyone who has been involved in my life proud by continuing to accomplish my goals that I set out for myself.

(Graduation picture I took for my bachelor's degree)

Eleven years old. The lucky number eleven? Eleven from
the show *Stranger Things*. Imagine making *the* decision that
would define your life when you were only eleven years old. On
top of that, you are not considered a teenager and have
extremely limited knowledge of life because of your race,
socioeconomic status, ethnicity, gender, sexual orientation, etc.
Let me guide you through my chapter of memories. For whoever
you are reading my story, I highly recommend you bring an open
mind so that you can have a dialogue with me. I am hoping that
you might understand the world from a distinct perspective,
where things can hopefully be more "just."

I am Jose. Also known as "Ache" or "Chepe" by my family, sometimes by my last name with my best friends and others by my middle name back in my home country. My pronouns are he/him/his/el. I was born in El Salvador, one of the smallest countries in America. Aha! Did I just make you question my previous sentence? Well, America is a continent, not a country. Always remember that and pass that knowledge on to others. Americans are people who were born on the American continent. Do not exclude everyone else. It is a topic for another time. For right now, let us continue.

At the age of eleven, my family and I decided to migrate to the United States. I had all the luck in the world because coming here was such a personal decision. I said *luck* not because I was privileged in the sense of having money where I could just decide to go wherever in the world and afford a luxurious life, but because I have amazing parents with an open mind. My parents allowed me to make the decision for myself – would I want to move to the United States – and from that moment there has been a phrase that has guided me through my journey. My motivational phrase is *"¡Hasta la victoria siempre!"*

I am not the only one in this world at the age of eleven to have taken *the* decision of their life, one in which I was asked to put my imagination and childhood aside. I am not the only one who has made the decision of an adult. It takes courage to start a life in an unknown country and there are many just like me who have taken the decision to move to another country. A country where the requirement to learn a new language can be a scary barrier. A country, where the colonizer culture continues to actively stop other cultures from bringing their *sazón* and holding onto or reclaiming cultures that others have tried to erase through genocide. I continue to struggle to adapt and sometimes I wonder if I will ever adapt here. *Soy inmigrante.*

Tuesday, February 28th, 2006. Where were you on this date? Were you born yet? Do you remember the year? Was there anything specific or exciting that happened in your life? I remember that night as if it was yesterday. It would be the last night I would see my friends from the neighborhood. It would be the last time I would play *fútbol* in the streets with goals made of stones. It would be a night of goodbyes, of jumping rope, playing tag, and hide-and-seek. It was a goodbye filled with complexity that I could not fully understand at the age of eleven. In my heart, I was still holding onto the hope that I would return tomorrow.

On that last night, I told my friends to look up at the sky at seven in the morning. I told them that they would see a large metal bird flying high. My flight heading to the unknown land of Los Angeles. To be honest on this last night, I cannot quite remember if there was a moon, but I do remember the stars cheering me up with hope for a better future.

It was a hectic night. My family was running errands and packing bags. I remember voices saying, "¡Pesá las maletas!" "Quítale cinco libras." "Tráeme el queso." Think about your experience when you pack for a vacation. You must decide what to pack, how to be efficient with the space in your bags. Now, imagine packing to move to a place where you don't have a home waiting for you. Most of my belongings, my prized possessions, would not be making the move with me. It was physically, emotionally and mentally draining.

Through all the chaos and late hours of the day, the two babies of the family had fallen asleep, my two cousins who would come and hang out every weekend. How would they feel if they didn't visit me anymore? How would they understand the reason why I was leaving? It is something I still wonder and have never gotten to ask.

"Elige sólo un *peluche.*" I had to pick my SpongeBob stuffed animal, a key chain! The only size that would fit in my bag with all that we would carry with us. My dog, a Siberian Husky with sky blue eyes, seemed to be the only one that really knew how my childhood home in El Salvador was going to change. He knew that he would not be able to look for me, my mom and my sister. There would be an emptiness painted by silence and nostalgia with our departure. The night was long, and tears and emotions emerged from even the strongest family member, my grandmother.

In a flash, I blinked, and it was four in the morning. I slept for three hours. I remembered that I would not see the sunshine one last time through the windows of my house. My small and beautiful home that gave me my imagination of everything I could become in the future was left in the darkness of the morning.

Wednesday, March 1st was leaving behind part of my childhood. March 1st was a sunny day, but deep down it was an electrifying storm full of emotions. On March 1st at five in the morning, I was close to the international airport of Comalapa, now known as San Oscar Arnulfo Romero y Galdamez International Airport. I did not cry when I said goodbye to the women who raised me, or the family to whom I was a little brother, a cousin, a son or a nephew. I just hugged everyone, and it felt like I would see them again, tomorrow. I took my backpack with clothes, walked with my mother and sister and passed by the cold,

frightening security checkpoint. You know, it is interesting because up to this day, I still get this feeling when I walk through a metal detector. It is a trauma that walks me back to March 1st, 2006.

I do not know how my mom had the courage and the strength to walk through this door. Maybe it was my sister's smile drawn out of melancholy. Maybe it was my innocence that gave strength to my mom. Maybe our ignorance of how life is for an undocumented immigrant in the United States. Or maybe just the possibility for us to survive.

The Journey of 3,000 Miles in Air.

The waiting was long until the metal bird was ready to

extend its wings through the sky. I think my age might have played a role in why it felt so long, but the reality was that we had been in the airport since five in the morning. I kept asking my mother impatiently when we would finally take off. I was nervous,

excited, and happy to fly. I still question why I was not feeling sad. Maybe it was because flying was something I had always wanted to experience.

My sister kept hugging my mother. A tear or two reflecting the windows from the airport and the reflection of a strong woman knowing the responsibility that she had to start a new life to provide to her children. Can you imagine if my mother had not had my sister there? Although she was still young, my sister understood the complexities of our decision and was someone that my mom could talk to. Although my mom was *the* adult, and was the strong one, I saw her be vulnerable with us, especially my sister. It is hard to be strong when you are about to pursue the life of an undocumented immigrant.

The speaker from the waiting room finally announced our boarding. We were called in order, and I got the window seat on the right side of the plane. I kept looking out. I was excited! I had come to the airport many times to pick up or drop off family members and now I was finally on the other side, inside of the airplane. We had invited my family to see our plane leave. There is an area of that airport where you can see all the planes departing and arriving. My dad used to take me there every time we went to the airport together. I tried to spot my family, but it was impossible. We put on our seatbelts and went through all safety procedures. The plane was ready to depart. Depart my *Pulgarcito de América*, a nickname for El Salvador as being one of the smallest countries in America. Depart from all the land I never got to visit and the land that I did. Depart from my family and beautiful memories.

For the first time, I experienced a force that pushed me to the back of my seat. As this force pushed me back, my mother and my sister began to cry, a crying like I have to this day never seen in my life. It scared me and I felt a powerful desire to console them. My mom hugged me, my sister hugged me, and I looked back to the window. We were now up high in the sky. Again, I could not understand why my mother was crying so hard. It hurt me seeing their tears erasing their makeup. I looked out of the window; I looked down and got distracted by the landscape. In those moments looking out of that metal bird, I realized how beautiful my country was (and is).

The landscape was breathtaking! A majestic river that ran behind the airport to the Pacific Ocean was an elegant blue. Further west I could see the beach *Costa del Sol*. My mom had calmed down and was telling my sister not to cry. *"Todo va estar bien hija. No llores por favor."* I cannot imagine the emotional and mental capacity that my mom had to be able to tell that to my sister, knowing that for however she felt, every tear they both cried held validity.

I looked down again and I saw the first volcano. I knew this was the San Salvador volcano. A lot of you might wonder how I knew. The logical explanation would be because we were heading towards Guatemala. Geographically, this is the first volcano that we would pass. The reason why I remember, though, is because I remember seeing many planes fly by my house. My house was close to the volcano (it was behind us). El Boquerón is the San Salvador Volcano. El Boquerón was a place that we frequently visited the last days before we left El Salvador. I loved going to El Boquerón because the air was a bit fresher. The land was filled with flora and delicious coffee plants. I always feared volcanoes because of their amazing power. The lava and the potential for destruction filled me with awe and respect. My curiosity was piqued when my family members visited the bottom of it! Every time we would go, my mom would tell me stories about how she climbed down with my cousins and my older brother. They would talk about how long it took them and how tired they were. To this day she still questions how they were able to do it. Well, every time we would go, I looked down, there would be some writing at the bottom, like a tag, and I always wanted to read it as I picture myself going down, too. When I was on the plane and looked down, I saw some of the writing inside, and I knew at that point this was El Boquerón.

Passing El Boquerón also meant that I was passing my home, my neighborhood, the *fútbol* field where I played many matches and the goals made with stones. I remembered what I told my friends and waved my hand to all of them, one last time. I still wonder if they went outside at 7 in the morning to look for me in the metal bird. I am still hopeful that one day I will connect with them again. When I do, I will ask them about that. I know I will be back.

After El Boquerón, I barely remember the rest of my country from that window. It feels like my mind has erased this memory as a safety mechanism to protect myself from feeling blue. Maybe I was too tired, but what I do remember is that in about 20 minutes, we were outside of Salvadoran land. I mean, it felt like I blinked twice or counted down 10 seconds. I finally realized how small El Salvador is.

My eyes slowly closed as I leaned into my mom's chest. Everything that happened that day felt like a dream. Where has time gone? Where was the moon? My brothers? My dad? Where was my godmother and my uncles, cousins, and friends? The window blind had begun to block my view and not very much later, I had already woken up from a quick nap marking that we were through the middle of our neighboring country, Guatemala.

Arrival at 12PM on March 1st:

How did I know that I was in beautiful Mexico? Well, since I lost track of time in the flight and kept slipping in between memories and sleep, there was something in the view that caught my attention. You see, if Latin America was one country, we would be the most beautiful country in the world. Starting with our people, we are one of the hardest working people. Latin America has all climates and landscapes. We would be one of the richest countries with the most natural resources. Our resources have been stolen for years as part of military operations, globalization, and imperialism led by specific people from the most powerful countries. I cannot blame entirely the people of the United States or from other developed countries as to why the world has been unfair to the Latin American region. But I can say that you, as part of a "democracy" or you as part of your government, need to wake up! There is a reason you live in a country that has everything! Have you questioned how you or your fellow citizens still find yourself living paycheck to paycheck when all these greedy people are making so much money? Money that they squeeze out of you and have time and time again stolen from other countries. It is time to wake up! No more! We all deserve a just way of living and you, as part of their regime, must also return what has been stolen from us.

Back to the memories of that day. When I looked down, I saw the beautiful Sonora desert from Mexico. What a landscape! With miles and miles of silent land and a radiant brown and maroon, it was like nothing I had ever seen before. As an 11-year-old kid, I had goosebumps and I imagined how scary it would be to walk in a lonely space without water and in a heat so dry it could kill. I am grateful for my life, for my parents and the privilege that my trip through the desert was only a few minutes. I was aware as a kid that many people traveled through that

117

desert to come to the United States. I could not and cannot begin to imagine spending days or sometimes weeks in a desert that deceivingly looks so beautiful from the sky. I knew the desert was the location of some of the worst and inhumane conditions that my undocumented community experiences on their way to the United States. I closed my eyes again and slept with fear.

I finally woke up to quite a different landscape. Can you guess how I knew I was in the United States? Snow. I woke up to the mountains of the San Bernardino Valley, not that I knew that was the name when I was 11 years old, but I saw bright snow that decorated the peaks like chocolate ice cream with coconut milk. The only thing I could think of was wanting to touch the white caps. I could not believe that I was seeing snow for the first time. In El Salvador, I would never have imagined seeing snow ever in my life. The plane started to slow down as it prepared to land in a monstrous airport that looked like a city itself. We landed at exactly 12:05PM. We had gotten safely to the United States.

Do you know what 12:05PM meant to me? 12:05 meant I needed to be mentally ready to confront homeland security if they asked me a question or put me in a room for hours. I had been trained to answer like a kid but with the confidence of an adult. I had been prepared to say that we had come to visit as tourists and go to Disneyland, "The happiest place in the world." It was our strategy to enter the United States without them suspecting that we had come to stay in the country. 12:05 meant we would carry the heavy luggage that carried our lives and personal belongings from El Salvador. 12:05 meant confronting the looming question, could my mother really get us through TSA? Would TSA really believe her English? 12:05 meant that TSA could have denied our entry because our visas were close to expiring. Would they let us come in? 12:05 meant hoping that my sister was not too nervous. 12:05 meant that my mother's picture and fingerprints were going to be taken and recorded. At 12:05 part of my childhood immediately died, and it was time to experience "real life." When the TSA check was over, I saw a smile from the corner of my eye. I could tell my mom had accomplished her first goal as an immigrant. They gave us up to 6 months to stay. It felt like all planets were aligned and there was a positive energy emulating from the three of us that convinced the federal agent we would be good citizens of this country.

We quickly moved to pick up our bags and, of course, we were lost. LAX felt like miles and miles of airport stretching in every direction. We had never seen such a huge airport where you could easily get lost. The mother of my aunt-in-law picked us up. Happy that we made it, her loud energy full of cheers and laughter reassured us that we were not alone and that we were finally with family again. My breakfast or should I say, brunch was some orange juice with Honey Bunches of Oats with Almonds.

Finding Home in the United States:

March 1st flew by. We were in the metropolitan city of Los Angeles until Sunday, four days in total. My aunt that lived in LA was incredibly happy to have us in her apartment. We could not really do much until she got home, but we walked around in the area, exploring the surroundings. It was cold or maybe it was just us, but in many ways, I was freezing during those four days. It is weird experiencing a cold like that for the first time. It is a type of cold that does not let you shower or bathe. A cold that keeps you glued to the sheets and although it was about 60 degrees, for me it was a difference of almost 25-30 degrees Fahrenheit from the tropical weather of my *Pulgarcito*. One of the first things I tried in the United States was walking in the crosswalks. You might be asking yourself, why? To me it was a big deal. My dad had always told me that people in the United States respect traffic signs. In El Salvador, you had to time yourself to be able to cross a street and you had to run. Drivers would not always respect crosswalks and it was always frightening. The morning of March 2nd, I walked down to the crosswalk and saw a car approaching the stop sign. The person in the car gave me the right to cross and, scared to death, my feet started walking cowardly looking around for any other cars until I finally got to the other side of the crosswalk. I was amazed by how safe I felt afterwards. Something so simple made me feel and understand that things were going to be super different here.

I reflected for a while on what I was going to accomplish and that one of those accomplishments would include going back to my beautiful *Pulgarcito*. I crossed the crosswalk one more time and went back inside to tell my mother about my adventure.

All through our time in LA, we ate delicious food. LA has an immense variety of foods. I challenge you to think of a food that you cannot find in LA. It is not just a matter of the variety, but how much more affordable it was compared to other places that we later visited. On top of that, back in 2006, everything was so much more affordable than it is now.

What I did not think was affordable though was Disneyland. Back in 2006 the entrance to Disneyland was $75! Everything inside was no less than $15 dollars. Advertised as "The Happiest Place on Earth." This place was and continues to be a debt trap, a savings eating monster for many families. I had the privilege to visit Disneyland on Saturday, the day before leaving LA. It had been a place I'd dreamt of visiting and I really wanted to go! I had seen the T.V. commercials in my *Pulgarcito* and it was literally a dream. I really wanted to see the castle. There are so many things to see and do in LA, but my family really wanted to grant me the opportunity to see Disneyland. And deep down, I know my sister was excited to visit, too. When we got there, I could not believe the price to just get in. It was ridiculous how much money we had to spend on entrance, on food, on anything and everything throughout the day at the park. If it were more affordable, maybe it could earn the title of "The Happiest Place on Earth" back. Anyway, as a kid who was beginning to feel like less of a kid and more of a pre-teen, I did not find this place full of the advertised magic and delight. First, the lines were extremely long. Rides were boring except for the Rocky Mountain Railroad roller coaster. I had never been on a ride like that before! Disneyland seemed like it was for little kids or adults who just had little kids. Maybe it would have been more fun if we had also gone to the other side, California Adventure. But of course, that would have been yet another expense.

At the end of the day, we made it the best experience and enjoyed seeing some of my favorite characters from the Disney movies. I was finally able to see Alice in Wonderland, my absolute favorite! I was grateful to be able to visit. I was grateful to be reminded that I was still a child despite all that had transpired in the last few days. That it was okay to still like to watch cartoons and embrace my imagination. We left Disneyland super tired and the next day we were ready to take the bus to the Bay Area.

It was Sunday and we woke up at six in the morning. We got ready and had a good breakfast. By 8AM, we were ready to leave my aunt's apartment and by 8:15 we were at the bus station. It was such a beautiful bus station with grapevines growing through the open wooden ceiling. It was another heartbreaking goodbye since we would not see my aunt for a while. We unloaded the huge suitcases that now had less stuff, having left some things with my aunt. The bus arrived at 8:30AM. We loaded our cases onto the bus. We were one of the first ones to pick a seat. There were three of us, so we had to separate during this leg of the trip across the two seats of the bus rows. My mom sat in a seat behind us, and my sister was next to me. At 9AM, we took off and we slowly said goodbye to the city of Los Angeles.

As we traveled through Highway 5, it was interesting seeing all the landscapes. As we went further and further inland, the landscapes transformed into more rural scenes of California. That was the second time I felt lost and lonely. I do not understand why we associate a cloudy day with sadness but that is exactly how this trip was. There was a melancholic breeze that seemed to be moving through my body as I watched fields and expanses of land without a sign of a single person walking around. That is how I knew how different the United States was from my *Pulgarcito*. There was no welcoming warmth from that scenery.

Three hours later, we made our first stop. I was able to use the restroom because I had been waiting to pee. I believe we were in Bakersfield when we had the opportunity to eat something. My mom had prepared some chicken salad sandwiches which calmed the hunger. We were stopped for a total of one hour. It felt so long and tiring to be sitting down for a long time. I did not even feel like going outside for long because it was such a cold day. Again, a difference of almost 30 degrees felt like a punch to the face. Fortunately, my brother from El Salvador had given my sister his Walkman and we had CDs with music that we listened to during the stop. My sister and I spent a lot of time listening to music and trying to sleep whenever we could.

As our bus ride continued through the solitude of agricultural fields, the only thing I could think of was wanting to get out of the bus to cut some fruit. My mom has passed onto me her love of picking fruit. Many people in the United States have fruit trees and yet prefer to buy the same fruit in supermarkets, letting the fruit on their trees rot. If anything, that should be illegal. I mean, it is food gone to waste. I wish things could be more sustainable, but maybe it is a reflection on the United States and their greed, wastefulness and gluttony. The bus stopped a couple more times, which allowed us to stretch. We finally got to the city of San Jose at 4PM. I felt such a relief seeing people in the streets. The bus driver announced that we were an hour away from our destination, but that we would wait an hour to leave.

We left San Jose at 5PM and around 5:45 we were arriving at the beautiful suspension bridge of the Bay Area. While I stared at the humongous bridge, I kept asking if this was the Golden Gate Bridge. It was interesting because some of the metal from the bridge looked red, so I thought that maybe because of the exposure to water from the bay, the bridge had lost its color. I was a bit scared of going over that bridge. I had never crossed one that was more than a couple meters in length or anywhere near as tall! Of course, the first thing you imagine is the worst-case scenario. To be honest, sometimes, I still get scared of bridges. Maybe I have a phobia of heights. This bridge is long and as we were crossing it in the bus, my sisters' Walkman played a classic instrumental jazz song that made me feel like I wanted to swing dance -- I don't even know how to swing dance! I felt chills through my body as San Francisco began to take shape outside the window. San Francisco greets you with tall skyscrapers as you cross the Bay Bridge. The bus finally arrived at the station at 6PM. It was starting to get dark and, of course, the cloudy skies did not help the lack of illumination.

When we got out of the bus, I looked up at the sky and I was immersed in the labyrinth of skyscrapers jutting up into the sky. I felt dizzy and a bit disconnected from what was happening next to me on the ground. A man passed in front of me. As I regained my focus from the sky, I saw that it was my uncle here to pick us up. I am not exactly sure how our luggage was able to fit in his minivan, but that thing felt like it was about to scrape its tires to the fenders.

We finally got to my aunt's home. It was such a nice neighborhood, calm and quiet. I didn't even want to think about unloading our luggage, so we first went to say hi to everyone. As soon as the door was opened the first thing that I heard was, "*primo*!" My cousin was super excited to see me. My aunt gave us a warm and rewarding hug.

I can't explain why, but my aunt's place always felt like a home to us. My aunt and the family made us feel like this should be the place to start and get settled. I felt happy being with my cousin knowing that he had toys with which I could play. My cousin had so many movies. I remember that first night, I saw a Star Wars lightsaber for the first time, and as you can imagine, we started to battle. Again, I could be a kid.

What is interesting is that my cousin was not just like any other cousin. My cousin quickly taught me to not be afraid to try to speak English or at least try to understand. Although my cousin has mental disabilities, he really challenged me because English was really the only language that he would speak.

A week after, my aunt and her family took us to our next and final destination to start our lives as Immigrants. We went back to the Central Valley in California. The city where we resided had a very lonely, rural feeling and was like a town in an old Western. Back in 2006, this was a land with limited opportunities. I think what was the most shocking about this city was the fact that everything looked like agricultural fields and most of its population were Mexican.

There was not a lot of diversity among Latines and although we are able to identify quickly with Mexican culture, there were some stark differences such as the slang that they spoke. Our accents were different and sometimes we faced discrimination because we didn't speak like them. There were differences in our cultures and traditions, and it felt like we could not be ourselves or embrace the fact that we were Salvadorans; we were looked at as inferior.

Our arrival was at my aunt's apartment. Now, let me be clear about something. My success, our foundation, the building blocks of my life in the United States are all thanks to my aunt from the Central Valley. Believe it or not, because of her we were able to execute our immigration plan. Because of her, we had a home when we arrived. Because of her we had food, and our transition was easier. Because of her, I was able to enroll in school and know the system that I know now. She and her family were our first building blocks. Although it was a tough place, she provided us the opportunity to do something with our lives here in the United States.

I remember arriving and feeling disconnected. If anything, I felt homesick and a bit disappointed. In El Salvador, everything felt happier. This city in the Central Valley was a depressing place. It felt hard to be optimistic. My aunt gathered up the entire family to welcome us. We ate amazing food. That afternoon as the time passed, everyone started to leave and head to their respective homes and that included my aunt from the Bay Area. When she left, I remember hearing a voice screaming inside of me, "Please don't leave us here." The scariest night I ever experienced in my life was that of our arrival. It was a day full of emotions. After moving our luggage and preparing for bed, I turned the light off and although it was just the light, something you can physically see, it was also something that I felt. It was a pitch black that my eyes never adjusted to. Darkness, like a black hole. At least the galaxy has stars, but this darkness scared me. A hopelessness hung in that darkness that made me hold onto my mom as my sister pleaded with her to sleep in the middle. March 12, 2006, is a moment in time that I will always remember and that made me fearful of being alone.

One More Stop to Find Opportunities:

It was a total of four months in this solitary land. The following week after we arrived, my mother, my aunt and my sister started to make decisions about the next part of our story here, putting down roots. Besides, of course, starting to find a job, my mother wanted to enroll my sister and me in school so that we could start learning the language. Can you believe that after all the traveling we had done across the state, we were lost in a language that we could not understand. I could speak my native Spanish language, but I was limited in how, where, with whom I could communicate and socialize. For an 11-year old kid, the only thing I could think about was how I was going to talk to other students at school. One of the stops was at the local elementary school. We got the registration information from the school's front office. I felt a little uncomfortable about the fact that I was going to be in fifth grade, again. The education system in the United States is hugely different from the education system in El Salvador. Besides all the discipline and subjects that we are taught, the school years start, break, and end at different times.

In El Salvador, the school year begins towards the middle of January and ends in late October. In the United States, you attend school from mid-August to June of the following year. Of course, you get days off during the Holidays, but they prioritize ending the school year as summer begins. Summer is the time to take advantage of the climate and being outside in the U.S.

As you can imagine, since it was March, the school year only had four months left so it made sense that completing fifth grade again was the best option, otherwise I would lose an entire year of my education in sixth grade. We also visited the local middle school. I was glad that I did not attend this school. It looked so sad and like a jail with its security gates. Lastly, we stopped at the local high school where my sister would be enrolled to start as a sophomore. The high school looked much nicer, but to me at that age, it looked intimidating since everyone was so much older. I ended up attending the local elementary school. Although I felt anxious, it was a much nicer school, and it had a more cheerful, less prison-like appearance and feeling.

My aunt helped my mom with purchasing school materials and a backpack. When the day came, my aunt and my mom went to drop me off at school. They took me to the front office and told the administration staff that I was new as she was completing some paperwork. The school called two kids so that I could start socializing, but to be honest they were noticeably quiet and that did not help me. I felt like a *pollo comprado.* It felt like everyone knew what was going on, where to go, and how to do this school thing except me. I cannot remember the name of the kids, but I do remember that they left me during the morning. I am not sure if they left me because they did not want to be with me or because they actually lost track of me. The good thing though is that I was able to find the room for my first class. I was fortunate that my first teacher in fifth grade was a native Spanish speaker. She was from Bolivia and was happy to welcome me to the school and that I came from another part of America.

My teacher introduced me to the entire class, and everyone was friendly. It was a bilingual class that was being offered to the top students from the school. Half of the time they had class in English and the other half they had class in Spanish. It was super cool to see students using both languages. At that time, I could only dream of being able to speak English fluently just like my Spanish. When the day finished, I was able to make some friends and the next day I felt much better attending school. I felt the courage to take the bus, but also that was my only option. My mom had prepared some food and snacks and we walked to the bus stop. I remember my mom saying, *"tú puedes hijo y recuerda que tu educación te va a llevar lejos. A seguir adelante."* Although I was only a fifth grader, my mom had talked to me like I had a big responsibility. She told me that I could do it and to remember that my education would take me far. She emphasized to keep moving forward. She stood at the bus stop waiting for the bus as the other kids walked by themselves. Fortunately, the bus stop was close to where we lived. It was only a block and a half away. My mom gave me a kiss before I got on the bus and then disappeared into the distance waving her hand with a hopeful face.

While I was at elementary school, I got to say that although it was a nice transition by having Spanish speaking friends, I was not really learning English. Most of my assigned books that I was reading were in Spanish. I remember that I had an assignment where everyone picked a state and they had to write and illustrate the history of a state. My state was California. This could have been an opportunity to practice my English, but the assignment was in Spanish. I was not learning any English. As time went by, I was introduced to another teacher that was from Honduras, Mrs. RO. She asked me if I wanted to come to the library with her twice a week to learn English. I told her that it would be helpful because I was not really learning. She was super happy to know that I was another student from Central America and because of her, I was able to make some progress.

During my learning time with Mrs. RO, we practiced basic words. It was so much fun because although it felt easy, I could feel myself learning. We had quizzes and small assignments. It was somewhat of a 1 to 1 learning, and she would also read to me. Towards the end of the year, Mrs. RO recognized me with my first certificate. It was a quite simple certificate recognizing me for my success and engagement in learning English. When I came home, I gave my mom the certificate and kept it on the wall as a motivation to achieve more. This would be the first of many certificates, awards, and honors I would earn.

During my time at elementary school, I got to visit Calaveras National Park and for the first time I saw sequoias, which left me in awe at how tall they stood. I mean, they were huge! We also went to Monterrey, an interesting experience. Not because I was visiting a new place, but because many of the kids in my class had never visited the ocean. They were impressed by how large it was. Me being from El Salvador, I was used to seeing the beach, but what was new was seeing the light-colored sand. The sand in El Salvador is a dark gray. As you can imagine, these are some of the things that I immediately told my mom when I arrived back home that day. I am sure my mom could not begin to picture the things that I had seen, but I felt a sadness in wishing that she and my sister could have been with me to visit.

During this entire time, my sister was adapting to the situation in her school. She made a friend that was super cool. She was from Jalisco and they both used to run track and field. My mom on the other hand was trying to find a stable and better paying job. She tried her hand at being a cook. I remember her buying dozens of eggs to practice flipping them in the kitchen.

My mom had the advantage of being bilingual, but it did not seem to make finding a job any easier. There were not a lot of places to apply to and most required some form of transportation. The bus system in the city where we resided was awful. I mean, the bus schedules did not make sense and walking to the bus stop could take you at least 30 minutes. It was a city meant for car transportation and unfortunately my mom had never learned how to drive. I do not know how my mom made it all that time, but summer was quickly approaching and that meant that cherry season was coming.

Graduation of Fifth Grade:

Guess what!? I graduated! In June of 2006, I graduated from elementary school, and I got a diploma. I felt weird because I had just arrived at the school, but I graduated! I wished my mom would have been able to see me at my graduation but because of work responsibilities she had to miss the ceremony. The last day of school was a minimum day, which was abnormal. My sister had already completed the school year and she was free to pick me up, but that is not what ended up happening. Many of my classmates were in actual suits and wearing semi formal dress clothes. I asked myself how I had missed the memo. I never thought that they had graduations for fifth graders. In El Salvador, things were completely different, and you would have to wait until high school to graduate, so you had about 11 to 12 years depending on your high school track before you would graduate. Though on the last day of school I took my favorite shirt and pants. I did my hairstyle like the wave, trying to look as handsome as possible. I realized when I got to school that I was again a *"pollo comprado."* Lonely and standing out in the middle of the crowd, I was wearing my everyday clothes at the ceremony of my fifth-grade graduation. I remember wishing that I had a pair of formal clothes to celebrate that milestone.

Since many parents went to see their kid's graduation, they gave the parents the option to take them home. The entire class left campus. I told my teachers that I had no one to pick me up. They tried to contact my mom to pick me up but that was not a possibility. They called my aunt's place, and no one answered because she was working. To be honest, I think the only way they were able to contact my sister was because we had a house phone and I had memorized the phone number. I asked my sister if she could do me the favor of picking me up at school. My sister had told me that she was going to try to pick me up but that she was not sure if she could. The school was a long walk from our apartment.

Time passed as I sat at school. I thought my sister was going to be able to pick me up, but time continued to pass by, and it was then the end of a normal school day. After waiting and waiting but never hearing back that someone was picking me up,

I ended up taking the bus. When I got home, I asked my sister what had happened. Annoyed, she recounted how she had gone to the school to pick me up and was told that she could not do so because she was not an authorized person. She had to walk back home again angry and in disbelief as the school personnel had not only been short with her, but wary and suspicious of her presence at the school.

The day passed, it felt nice that we were no longer in school and now I had to prepare for middle school. For some reason though I was nervous, but since I had begun to acclimate, I was ready to take on the challenge of middle school. I had made some friends at school and many of them were going to the same middle school as me, so that made me more confident and actually a little bit excited.

Fútbol World Cup, Germany 2006:

I promise there is a reason that I am bringing this up. My sister and I were on vacation as were some of the other kids in the apartment complex. One Sunday, I remember that there was a family party going on and they were playing Mexican Loteria. It is like Bingo for the United States, but with more *sazón*. I had been feeling very lonely and there were some kids playing outside. I worked up the guts to ask if I could play with them.

They were very welcoming. I had finally made some friends in the apartment complex! My friend was very cool, and he had a lot of cool games. He had a PlayStation and invited me a couple times to play with him. I had not played video games since I left El Salvador. We also used to play *fútbol* in the parking lot. It was during this time that I got particularly good at controlling the ball.

My friend and his family later moved to another apartment away from the upstairs section and they were at the opposite end of the apartment complex. But since we were one of the few kids, we would always go outside and play *fútbol*. During this time, the world cup in Germany started and we watched many of the games. Luckily, we bought a rabbit ears antenna, and we were able to get the local channels. We did not have many, but at least we could watch the world cup on channel 14. During this summer season, my mom started working in the cherry fields. This was something that people always waited for in the summer. It was physically demanding work, but it was a secure way to make money; they paid minimum wage for those long hours.

One of our neighbors worked at the cherries. She had a car. The cherry fields were far from where we lived, about an hour and a half away. Our neighbor had offered my mom to always give her a ride to work. My mom would help with gas money to divide costs.

Working picking cherries or sorting cherries lasted only a month. My sister and my mom both decided to begin working.

There were a couple of other minors that would work during this time, although it was not permitted. Some of the tough things about working in this job was that you had to wake up extremely early and you would come back super late. I mean, my mom would wake up at 4AM and come back at 8PM. When both my mom and my sister were working, they would both be gone for extended periods of time. I would stay by myself and play with what was around. I did not have many things to distract myself with, but I would for sure watch the games and try to find cartoons to watch.

One evening after they had both gone out to work, my mom and my sister came back exhausted. It was a rough day, and it was also a scary one. Authorities know that many of these places hire minors without work permits. On this day, the authorities arrived at the place to check if they were hiring minors. My sister along with other kids had to run and hide amongst the cherry trees. She had so much adrenaline pumping through her veins as she ran and hid. After that day, she still chose to go back to work. She got paid, but they told her not much later that she could not come back to the fields anymore; they were afraid of getting into trouble.

My sister began staying with me again and we continued watching the world cup together. One night, on the last day of cherry sorting, my mom did not appear to be coming back. It was late and my sister and I started getting worried. We tried calling our neighbor, but she would not respond. There was no signal out in the fields where my mom was working. Of course, the first thing your mind jumps to when something like this happens is if there has been an accident or that *la Migra* (I.C.E) had shown up and searched the place. It was not until 11PM that she appeared at the front door. My friends from the apartment complex were with us until the very last minute when my mom finally arrived. We hugged her for a long time. I felt so safe to be in the arms of my mom. We were together, again.

A week after, the world cup final was soon approaching, and my mom had proposed the idea to visit my aunt in the Bay Area to spend some time with them. My aunt came to pick us up on July 8th of 2006. My mom had told me that we were going to visit for 2 weeks and that later we would come back to the Central Valley.

I had mixed feelings about visiting. Not because I did not want to spend time with my aunt and family, but because I was finally adapting to the neighborhood and wanted to spend time with my friends there. I started to ask myself if I would still have the same friendship with my friends from the apartment complex. If they were going to forget about me. I really was scared to lose what I had adapted to and had created for myself.

Well, we left for the Bay, and I quickly forgot that I had wanted to stay in the Central Valley. I was happy to see my cousin and my family again! I was able to play with him and all his toys. We watched many of the movies that I enjoyed, went to the neighborhood pool and played outside.

The world cup final was on July 9th. The golden game. The game the world waits every four years for, and this one would be the most watched. We were super excited to see the final between France and Italy. My aunt had Italy's blue shirt from the player Del Piero. Someone had gifted her the shirt, such a great gift. My aunt gave my sister the shirt to wear during the final while my family rooted for Italy, except my uncle who cheered on France.

The game began! France made the first goal in the first seven minutes of the game! Can you believe it! If you are rooting for a team and your team begins to lose within the first seven minutes, you begin to feel like your team has already lost the game, and you intentionally or not begin to settle in, accepting the fact that you are about to watch your team lose. Of course, there was a lot of time left and soon after, Italy scored and my aunt's house was filled with celebration, yelling and cheering. The regulation time was over, the 90 minutes of the game ended in a tie. It was such a close game. Both teams got close to scoring a winning goal, but it would not happen. The game continued into extra time and then into the nail-biting penalties, which has always been one of my favorite moments of a *fútbol* game. For a game to end with penalty shootouts added to the excitement of the day. Goal after goal after goal until

France missed a second goal! Italy continued and never missed a single shot. They became champions of the world! We all celebrated and jumped around the house until we realized that it was still early and that we could do more with the day. The day was an extremely hot one. One of those days you need to find shade to stay cool, so we decided to go to one of the local parks. It was such a beautiful park with tall redwoods and a refreshing breeze. It is that feeling that trees give you when the smell of pine needles fills your nose, and you are protected from the sunlight. There was a river of cold water that invited you to throw rocks and put your feet in. We celebrated Italy's victory with a carne asada and although we are not from Italy, we were happy for the game they played. True champions.

As the world cup ended, we still had quite some time to spend at my aunt's place. I mean, it was only the beginning of our vacation! They took us to visit more places in the Bay Area. We visited other state parks. As the time quickly passed, our vacation was coming to an end. I asked my mom if we were going back to the Central Valley, but when the day came, she said that we would stay another week in the Bay. I was very excited at her answer and having the time to play with my cousin. Now, that week became another week and another week until my mom told me that we were moving from the Central Valley. She told me, "*Hijo, lo he estado pensando y hable con tu tía de movernos para acá. Acá tendré más oportunidades de trabajo. Todo es más accesible y tu tía está dispuesta a ayudarno*s." This time I did not have a choice about going or staying, but I understood that my mom was doing what was best for my sister and me. I knew she was doing this for our future, and I could not argue with her regarding the accessibility and the opportunities of work.

I felt nervous and anxious again. I started thinking of all the progress we made in Central Valley and now we would have to learn, adapt and reacclimate all over again. I was nervous to go to a different school and feel like *"pollo comprado"* again. I knew this was a better choice, so I had to be brave and do my part. I never really asked my sister how she felt about this situation in so much detail, but we both agreed this was a good change. My mom, sister and I would share a bedroom for a while until we could get set to move out.

Soon after, my mom had to deal with canceling that contract from our apartment in the Central Valley and we had to figure out what to do with the things we had bought. Fortunately, one of our family members offered my mom his small garage to store all the things that we had. I know my mom had to give much of the stuff away, but we did save the essentials. I was feeling down when my mom went. I could not say goodbye to my friends, who had been so great to me and my family. Life continued and then it was time to prepare for middle school.

Welcome to Middle School:

It was the end of August in 2006. I enrolled in middle school.

The middle school that I enrolled in was close by and provided transportation. I remember the day before my sixth-grade orientation. When we drove by my middle school, I liked it more than the middle school in the Central Valley. It was much more welcoming. The visit made me feel excited about attending the new school. I kind of could not wait to go to school. The next day, my mom and I took the bus to my new middle school and attended the orientation. It felt weird walking into the gym for the first time. A lot of the people welcoming us were white and the only thing I heard was English. I went to register with my mom, but I could not find my name. I honestly thought they had used my second last name instead of my first, so I grabbed the registration that I thought was mine, unintentionally taking it from another kid who had the same last name.

Orientation was draining! For most of the time, I did not understand anything and to be honest I did not make any friends, so I was scared that my first day of school was going to be horrible. I was stressed about it until the day finally came. My mom, being the amazing and loving mom that she is, walked me to the bus station. My bus was the number three. It was the typical yellow bus with the egg yolk color. While waiting for the bus, I met a Peruvian kid who seemed to really know how the system worked and was a very extroverted person. He would prove later to be manipulative and annoying, but that is something that I did not know just yet. He was the first person who introduced me to middle school. He started to talk a lot with me and my mom while waiting for the bus. Not all kids looked happy to be getting picked up, but when we got to school, I was able to hang out with him for a bit and he showed me around the school. It seemed like he already knew people when we got there.

The bell rang and it was time to find my class. I had gotten my schedule along with the registration papers during the orientation, and so I was still going under the name that I gathered during orientation. I went to the classroom of Mrs. AN, the teacher for advanced ELD. When we all got to the class, although some people were speaking Spanish, a lot were speaking English. I sat down at a table and thought to myself that it was going to be hard to speak English, but I felt motivated to learn. We were going to begin to introduce ourselves, when another kid entered the room with one of the assistant principals. Can you guess who it was? Well, yes! It was the kid who belonged in the class, the student whose schedule was in my hands! This entire time I had been moving through school as if I was someone else, but when they came to find out who I was, I told them that I had the same name.

To solve the matter, the assistant principal took us both to the office to figure out which kid belonged in which class. I was anxious, crossing my fingers and hoping that I was the correct kid in Mrs. AN's class. Maybe I was the one in the right classroom. I kept saying to myself that I was going to be the right student, I was going to be the right student. Can you guess how they figured it out? They asked me for my full name and when they heard my first last name, I became the wrong kid. In the education system of El Salvador, they take into consideration your entire name. Here in the United States, it is only your first name and your first last name. When I searched for my name during orientation, I did not find my first last name, so I assumed that they had put me down with my second last name. This was a learning curve and here I was feeling like a *"pollo comprado"* yet again, not used to how things were done anywhere but in El Salvador.

Now that they knew who I was, they figured out that I should have been in Ms. PK. They walked me to her class, and it was quite interesting that she didn't know much Spanish as an ELD teacher. When I entered her class, it seemed like one, they had already gone through the rules of her classroom and two, she was speaking only English! She did not have any help from a teacher who would translate for her, so literally it was the students and her. I felt uncomfortable again being in another classroom where all the attention was on me. I mean, I disrupted the class just being who I was!

As we continued through the first period, I met a really cool person who was nice to me from the beginning. He was the first friend I made in middle school. BH was the person who helped me to adjust to Ms. PK's class. He would translate for me and although he was still a beginner, he understood more than I did for sure. Maybe he was misplaced in terms of his English-speaking level. During class we were learning about Dr. Martin Luther King Jr. That was the first time that I heard the "I Have a Dream" speech. I had no idea who he was or what he was saying in his speech, but he seemed like someone very important to the history of the United States, like a revolutionary. There was a break between first and second period and BH and I got to chat for a while. He had a funny hair style. We knew it as *la ola*. It was a very popular style during that time. Especially among newcomers. BH asked me where I was from and how long I had been here. He was cool and introduced me to other people.

When the bell rang for second period, I saw another teacher who was entering the classroom to observe Ms. PK and do assessments to specific students. I got called on by this teacher. Her name during that time was Ms. JM, which she later changed to Mrs. JZ. Mrs. JZ started asking me questions regarding how much English I knew. I told her that it was limited and that I only knew a couple words. This was true. I mean, I had taken some English classes in El Salvador, but at that moment I really did not remember much. She did some testing and then asked me if I would be interested in joining her class. I told her immediately "yes." Maybe because I felt that wherever I was going, it was going to be easier. Or maybe because she had taken interest in my learning and had shown she cared from even the first interaction. To this day, I still remember her because she was really the door for me to believe I could do any of this. She showed me that teachers can care for students to learn.

This is why it is important that our new generations continue to get an education. We must protect our teachers. Teachers do all this important work while parents are at work. They care for your children and teach them to prepare for success. Teachers do so many things for their students. They are therapists, counselors, mentors, coaches, nurses when you need a band aid or feel sick; they absorb the energy that students bring from home, healthy or not. Teachers are undervalued. More and more are required of them while salaries, which is an important component to their lives, don't reflect the work that gets piled on them! I see more people not wanting to be teachers nowadays while our government prefers to spend money in the military instead of allocating the budget for resources, sufficient staffing, and salaries in our schools, preparing our new generation with a just and high-quality education. Mrs. JZ was a teacher that you could tell got into the profession because she loved teaching, and she specifically loved teaching ELD. When I went to her classroom, there were only a couple students and most of us had limited to no exposure to English. She was very engaging and started teaching us very simple words. It really felt like an introduction. It felt amazing to be learning in the safe environment Mrs. JZ had created, where it was okay to make mistakes and she could always communicate with us in Spanish.

As the day went by, I noticed that I had more knowledge of English than I thought I had had. Maybe it was the classes that I took in El Salvador. Maybe it was the fact that I was learning from my cousin every day. Maybe it was what I had learned at my elementary school in the Central Valley or maybe the video games that I used to play when I was in El Salvador. To be honest, I am not sure, but because I felt so safe with participating and with learning, by the end of the day, Mrs. JZ talked to me and said that I was more advanced than this class level. She said that it would be better if I went to Mr. KR's class, who at that time was teaching the middle level for ELD. Technically this was a more advanced ELD course than Ms. PK's class. I felt motivated and nervous. I saw it in myself, and Mrs. JZ was right. I was going to learn more at the next level because everything that we were covering in her class was easier. Well, she talked to Mr. KR from room 10 and by the next day I was in his classroom feeling again like a *"pollo comprado."*

Meeting My Best Friend in Mr. KR's Class:

My mother was very happy that I was at a higher level for ELD. She completely supported me to challenge myself and told me that making these moves would allow me to continue going further and succeed in the United States. On that same afternoon of my chaotic first day, my mom took me to enroll in an afternoon school program run by one of the local nonprofits. I was not very happy about it. I was going to spend my entire days doing school related stuff. She told me it was going to be helpful as they were going to support me with my homework. I continued telling her that I was not interested and that I could do my homework at home. I did not need an afterschool program; but guess what! I did not have an option. We could not drive, so we had to walk, which was about 20 minutes from where we lived.

When we got to the place, we headed towards the administration offices where we were the only people asking for their services. The program would not start until the following week, so I thought to myself that I still had some time to hang out with my cousin during the afternoons and do other things. While my mom was filling out some paperwork, I sat down on one of their waiting area benches close to the window looking out at the street. Suddenly, two people entered the office. It was a lady and a kid about the same age as me. They told him to sit down on the benches in the waiting area while the lady who appeared to be his mother went to ask for information regarding the afterschool program, too.

I started to look at some of the books that were on a table, and I picked up *The Outsiders*. The kid approached me and asked if I had read the book. I told him no because the book was in English, and I had never heard about it before. He told me that it was a *chingón* book and he started telling me more about it. He later proceeded to introduce himself. His name was

JV. I introduced myself and he asked me what grade I was in and the school that I went to. During this entire time, I thought wow, this kid is cool. Very friendly and outgoing and very extroverted, while I was more introverted on the other hand.

My mom then called me as we had signed up and were now prepared to leave. I told him that it was nice to meet him. JV's mom asked my mom if we were also asking for information about the afterschool program. She went on to say that JV was getting enrolled as well and that we would see each other in the program. We said our goodbyes. I thought that this might be the first and last time I would talk to JV, so I didn't think too much about it again. I met my best friend on the first day of school, but not at school. Without *The Outsiders* laying on the table, I never would have met him. This is a memory we will always remember, and I cherish a lot.

As we walked back to my aunt's house, my mom was giving me all the directions on what to do for the afterschool program; where I would walk, when the bus would drop me off after school. I completely forgot about the idea of me wanting to stay home after school and had become more open to the idea of the afterschool program.

The next day, my mom walked me again to the bus stop, but this time she did not stay for the entire time. She just dropped me off and I told her it was okay, that she did not have to stay. My mom really liked spending time with me during the walk, but she also understood that it was important to spend this time to check on my mental health. She wanted to make sure that I was adapting well to the new situation. I took the bus, and I got to school early. Spent some time sitting down on the benches and when the bell rang, I headed to Mr. KR's classroom. I don't know exactly how I communicated, but I gave him my schedule and got him to understand that I was new, and that Mrs. JZ had sent me to his room.

When I entered the classroom, I realized that the Peruvian kid, the one who I met on the bus, was also in this class. I also realized that JV, my soon-to-be best friend, was in the classroom. The other people were new faces though and some students definitely looked way older than me. This was the thing about Mr. KR's classroom, we were from all different grades. I sat in the back and when class began, I quickly realized that this was way more challenging than I had prepared myself for! It was *all* English and I could not understand almost anything that was going on. The good thing was that we did have a teacher who would translate for us. She was Mrs. AM. Both teachers were strict but were very nice and always wanted to help students to achieve their full potential.

The very first classes with Mr. KR were difficult. I was in his classroom the entire time. He was teaching me ELD, and he would also teach me Math. There were only about eight sixth grader students in his classroom and that is how I started to make more friends throughout the year. The day would always start with Mr. KR giving us a warm-up where we had to correct sentences. There were punctuation errors and grammatical errors. I remember I got called once and was not able to give an answer because I was super lost. My first progress report was not particularly good in English. I had a C average for ELD. Math on the other hand though was much easier. I was much more advanced in Math and I quickly became the top student. I used to love going to Math class because I would understand and feel successful.

To be honest, I think it was more thanks to Math class that I was able to demonstrate to Mr. KR and Mrs. AM that I was a disciplined and hardworking student. As you see, I did not use good or bad students. I also did not use smart students. I believe we are all smart and capable and there is no such thing as a bad or good student. If we look beyond the student and understand factors that affect their lives, we can begin to understand the influences and root of students' behaviors. I got to say, I was able to quickly

catch up to everyone's level as the time went by in the first school quarter. Quickly, I started to read beginner level books. Mr. KR always motivated me and because of him I transferred from doing my reading records from Spanish books to English books. I was learning! I was a sponge, and nothing could stop me.

The Sixth Graders:

I started to meet a lot of new people at the after-school program. During the program, we had the privilege to get help with our homework. We would work on community projects and every Tuesday we would stay until 7:30PM for a club that was either gender specific or mixed. I was in the boys and girls club just like JV. The program and the tutoring would be divided by newcomers and the other half would be students that already knew English.

One day while waiting for the program to start, I sat at one of the tables with another kid who was from El Salvador. This kid was hilarious and super hyperactive. I could immediately get his jokes as we spoke the same slang and his creativity with creating new jokes would just leave you lost in a world of incredulous confusion if you did not know the same slang terms. I mean, his brain had a split-second reaction time to concoct each new joke. This kid was EH. He was super cool, and we got along immediately. If I was looking to laugh, all I needed to do was find a seat next to him.

By now, JV, the Peruvian kid (GJ) and I would hang out in school and during the after-school program. One time when we arrived at the program, I told JV and GJ to sit with EH. This was the first time the sixth graders at the after-school program all hung out. But let me tell you that the sixth graders were not all four of us. It really only was EH, JV and me. We would always hang out and GJ would join us on occasion, while other times he would prefer to hang out with other people.

GJ always felt like he needed to be in control of everyone. I remember how cruel he could be to JV, that was something I never liked. He would smack you in the head, order you around, and he would try to take advantage of the fact that some of us could not speak English very well, yet. To be honest, GJ bullied JV and tried his best to do the same to me and EH. It was when he began to realize that he couldn't bully EH or me that he then chose to pick on JV. One time while we were all heading to the program, GJ was teasing JV and it got to the point that we were all fed up with his incessant comments and his physical aggressiveness. JV stood up for himself, with EH and me backing him up, of course. We told him to stop bothering us and that if he did not stop, we would make him.

This continued until we got all the way to the after-school program. Think about it, as a kid, standing up to a bully makes you feel big and courageous, and I remember feeling strong. We felt like brothers, we had each other's backs. We were unstoppable and without fear of bullies or really anything. GJ went to the supervisors saying that we wanted to beat him up. He even started crying. EH, JV and I got called to the main office where they said they were going to call our parents because we were "bullying" GJ. We stopped the supervisor in her tracks and told her what was going on and how he was the one bullying us. How EH, and I had stepped up because JV had had enough of GJ's bullying and how we had warned him to stop. GJ got called again to the office, and they agreed that GJ was the actual person doing the bullying. They called his mom while JV, EH and I continued with our day. On that day, JV, EH and I became really good friends, and we became *the sixth graders*. We were always together, all the time. I felt like I belonged to a group that I could call friends. I was accepted for who I was, and I accepted them for who they were. We all had different struggles, but we were happy starting our teen years.

A Race to Meet Another Best Friend:

I loved sixth grade as it progressed. There was always *fútbol* going on during the mornings, which meant that I got to show not only my skills with the ball but my talent for being fast at running. The news about my speed at running quickly spread and I was introduced to another kid, KM. KM was a runner. Everyone knew him as an amazingly fast kid. KM was not a super tall kid, but he was quick in comparison to everyone else. If anything, he was definitely one of the fastest kids at the school. Exceptionally talented.

About 10 minutes before the bell rang for the morning, we raced from some portable bathrooms to the baseball field fence. We agreed that we would race there and back. The distance was probably about 100 meters. The race was intense! It was hard to tell who was going to win. As I started reaching my maximum speed, I started to gain more distance in front of him, but he was still remarkably close. By the time the race ended, I was only about five meters from him. He was happy that he had found someone his speed and from that day we became friends, with a rivalry in running. It was immediately a relationship of respect because we both had talent. He told me he wanted to race me again later in the afternoon and we did. The result was still the same.

There was something that KM was better at than me. Although we never got to race this type of event until eighth grade, he was definitely a distance runner. When we would talk, we would compare our mile times. KM was always at least 30 seconds faster than my time. Every time I got faster, he got faster and although we were both close, KM was faster at distance running and I was faster at sprints. He encouraged me to join cross country but attending the after-school program made it so that I could not join. It was a race where I met one of my best friends and the person who always pushed me to new limits through running and academics.

My First Honor Roll and Visiting the Civic Center:

The first quarter in sixth grade had concluded. Grades were out and after all my discipline, hard work and adaptation to middle school, I achieved my first Honor Roll award! I had earned this in the category of A's and B's. To be honest, I was surprised because I was struggling so much in English and I hadn't been able to see the progress, but I had moved from a C to a B!

I guess attending the after-school program really had supported me and it wasn't only me but almost all the sixth graders from Mr. KR's class that earned Honor Roll. I can say that the common denominator was the after-school program. Mr. KR called our names in front of the class and made us stand up to congratulate us. Later, we went to the gym for a ceremony for achieving Honor Roll where they gave us donuts as a reward. After the ceremony, I told JV that we should propose the goal to always make it to the Honor Roll until the end of the year. This certificate was the start of a new chapter. It was a symbol of resilience. A symbol that a foreign language would not be a barrier and that I could achieve remarkable things.

Due to our accomplishment, all the sixth graders from Mr. KR's class got the opportunity to visit the Civic Center for a day. We spent an entire day learning from professionals and leaders in the community that worked at the Civic Center. We got to visit the courts and all the installations. Of course, most of the professionals that we were meeting were white but there was one person that stood out for all of us who attended the field trip. His name was DE. DE was an administrative aid to the former fourth district board of supervisors in the county. He talked to us in Spanish and English and he was from El Salvador! What was cool about DE is that he identified himself as an indigenous person of the Lenca-Potón Nation. As he spoke about his work and his identity, he was very motivated and happy to see us succeeding at school. I don't know about the other students, but I felt extremely proud to have found a person not just from El Salvador, but also a leader in the county who represented my indigenous people, the majority of whom had been assassinated by corrupt governments. El Salvador is one of the countries that has little indigenous people representation. DE told us to stay away from problems and to continue working hard so that we could join him in being leaders in the community.

I cannot deny how lucky I was. What I experienced in sixth grade motivated me to be disciplined and work hard at school. I had this hunger for success and to be the best student in the class. JV and I stayed out of trouble. We made it to honor roll the entire year and I also achieved recognition as the best student of the month, which was recognized in the entire school. I have the plaque with my name and the year. To this day, I continue to look at that plaque as one of my biggest achievements. It was proof that I was learning English. I sent a picture to my dad and kept him informed of my successes. If I remember correctly, I made him cry multiple times. Not tears of frustration or sadness, but tears of happiness. He was truly proud of my accomplishments.

A Family Reunion and Seventh Grade:

We made it to seventh grade. As the logic goes, since I

completed the mid-level for ELD, now it was time to move up to Advanced ELD class. I was back at Mrs. AN's class, but this time because I belonged there. It was kind of weird to think that I had made it to this level in only one year. If you had asked me a year before if I thought this was possible, I would have told you no. I realize now that I am very proud that I was able to get to this level so quickly. I have to give credit to my family, the teachers who supported my success, the after-school program, and also myself. I was and continue to be extremely hungry for success. Being in Advanced ELD also meant that I was one year away from taking regular classes in English. I was going to join everyone else like a native English-speaking student. My focus right then though was to complete seventh grade.

Before I continue to give you more details regarding seventh grade, I have to update you on what happened during September of 2006. When I was still in sixth grade, my brother made the decision to move to the United States. This is my second brother, and he did the entire trip by himself.

My brother did exactly what we did but instead of going to the Central Valley, he came to the Bay. He was given a six-month permit to stay in the country, like the rest of us. Unlike us, he had the advantage of having a driver's license in El Salvador. Even on a tourist visa, he could drive if he presented his paperwork to show that he was just visiting.

I was so excited to see my brother. There were tears in the eyes of all my family members. My sister felt the most supported by the presence of my brother. He also brought a different energy as he has always been a joker. He brought a levity with him that made everyone much happier. Now it was the four of us. My brother quickly became an emotional and financial support to the family. In many ways, I felt lucky that I had my older brother that would look out for me here. He was like a dad.

When my brother arrived, he quickly found a job and started working at a local pet store. My mom tried to find all kinds of jobs. She tried retail, making pizzas at a restaurant and she worked at a candy store. She never made a bad face about any of the jobs she tried. She always made it very clear that she had to do whatever she could to help us succeed. It got to a point when my mom could not handle having multiple jobs. It was not just her getting tired, going from one place to another, it was also exhausting for my brother to drive her to multiple places throughout the course of a day. My mom decided to nanny, and to this point she still does. My mom taught me a lesson very early on. She was a professional in El Salvador holding a position as an executive assistant for a bank there. My mom is a person that reads voraciously in both English and Spanish and thus has a very extensive vocabulary in both languages. She is to this day a walking dictionary to the family. When she got here, she never looked down on any job. I learned that no job is above another or below any other, and the people working them should always be respected with dignity no matter what. Everyone is essential. Unfortunately, we are all not recognized in this way.

For the next two years until 2008, the four of us continued to live under my aunt's roof in one of the bedrooms. We had no space for anything, but being close to my aunt, we always had a great time with her and the family.

The school year started, and I was going into seventh grade. My seventh-grade year was very successful. I earned Honor Roll the entire year and straight A's. I was successful in all my courses. Because I was now in Advance ELD, I had an elective course. My first semester, I had art and my second semester I took woodshop.

During this year, JV and I were best friends. Although we did not always hang out, we always had each other's back. EH on the other hand, started to hang out more with kids outside of the ELD classes, but he would still say what's up once in a while. KM began taking non-ELD courses during this time, so he also met new people. Everyone was everywhere, but we always maintained communication with each other.

For the second time, I got nominated as student of the month. I was nominated back-to-back in sixth and seventh. I was a very disciplined student, which I think gave peace of mind to my mother. She knew and trusted that I wouldn't get off course.

In 2007, my father decided to come visit us. I had left my home, El Salvador, only a year and half ago, but already I had changed so much. I had grown! I was going through puberty! My hair was long, and my voice was changing. When I left El Salvador, my dad knew me as a kid, a fifth grader, just 11 years old. When he got here, I was a young teen who had grown up with not only the passing of time but also the journey that I had pushed through to be standing here. I was now literally standing taller than him. He did not even recognize me. He continued to stare at me. I could see in his eyes that he was attempting to piece together how I had changed so much during the time we were separated. I never really realized how much I had grown since I came to the United States, but in that moment, I saw it in his reaction. My cousin and my grandmother also came to visit us from El Salvador. I was grateful that some family members had a visa and could make the trip.

In many other ways, 2007-2008, my seventh-grade year, was a difficult school year. My family is by no means perfect, and it was not a great day every day even with the addition of my dad to the four of us here. We had challenges still to face. I am not exactly sure how I was able to perform at school at the level I performed. When my father visited, there were continuous arguments between him and my mom that all came down to that fateful decision to come to the United States. My father had always opposed coming here because he knew how difficult life would be here and how hard it would be to adapt to a new culture. He was not wrong, but we couldn't continue living in El Salvador. From what I understood, our financial situation was going downhill.

In line with my father's concern, my sister began having a tough time adapting. She had it the hardest with respect to adapting and finding opportunities to succeed. My sister is the definition of resilience.

My sister was bullied during high school, which led her to drop out. She navigated through a toxic environment where both Latine and white students would bully her. It was cruel and a nearly impossible environment to learn a language. The staff at the high school never really put a stop to things. There were so many factors that impacted her during school, the absence of all the family, the absence of her friends from El Salvador, learning a new language, and dealing with bullying that deeply impacted her mental health.

As a family, it was our job to support her, and it was a pressure that I carried with me when I went to school. Was my sister okay? Would she be fine at school today? I was worried about her a lot during this time. My dad's visit was key to supporting my sister and the entire family. My brother was freed up for a while from taking my mother to her job.

My dad stayed for six months, and he decided to go back to El Salvador leaving us with the promise that he would return. He needed to fix some legal things regarding his business, so it was important that he go back. For the second half of seventh grade, and first half of eighth, my dad was absent again.

Out of ELD and Entering Eighth Grade:

It took two years before I started to finally have conversations fully in English. So many things had changed by the time I started my eighth-grade year. First, we had moved from my aunt's house. With the financial stability of my brother's and mother's jobs, we were able to move from sleeping all together in one crowded room to a slightly larger space. We moved into an apartment with two bedrooms. We could have our privacy again and start living life a bit more regularly. Life was feeling normal, and the best thing was that I could walk to school! I did not need to take the bus. It also meant that I could sleep more. Eighth grade was one of my favorite years in middle school.

Let me tell you a little about the move to our new apartment. We rented a UHAUL to pick up all the things that we had initially purchased in the Central Valley. Everyone took a trip there. Even my aunt from the Bay Area went. We also took the opportunity to visit family from the Central Valley and check on how they were doing.

You are not going to believe this. It had been more than two years! When we got to our Central Valley apartment, I came to find that our friends were not residing in the apartment complex anymore. At that point, I thought that I had completely lost contact with them. As we were showing my brother more of the surroundings of the apartment, a kid passed by the neighborhood on a bike. It was my friend! He was super happy to see me and quickly leapt from his bike to say hello. He took us to where he was now living, and we saw his family one last time. Then, we went to visit my sister's friend from Jalisco, and she welcomed us to a birthday party. We could not stay too long because our family was going to be worried, and it was also getting late to go back home. I was overjoyed that I was able to say one last goodbye to our friends. After that day, I never heard from them again. It is like a chapter in a book, you know. The people that I met along my journey were gone with the closing of different chapters, yet I still wonder to this day how they are doing and what they are up to. They were great people and without them, our transition to this country would have been so much harder.

We got back from picking up our things in the Central Valley and I began to settle into my eighth-grade school year. It was around this time that I started to even dream in English. At first, I found it odd that most of my conversations were now in English even while I slept. One of my favorite teachers was Mrs. BR. She was an amazing and caring teacher. One of those teachers whose lessons never leave you, even after you've left their class, staying with you for the rest of your life. Teachers like Mr. KR, Mrs. JZ, Mrs. AM, and Mrs. AN. These are teachers that our city, county, state and nation should be grateful to have or have had. Mrs. BR was a strict teacher but very cool. She deeply cared for JV and me. She knew we were hard workers, but she also understood that we were students and sometimes would joke around just like any kid our age. It was also one of my favorite classes because JV sat right next to me the entire year so we could joke around all the time.

I had History with *the* most strict and terrifying teacher on campus. You know who was lucky though? JV! He had Mr. TK! One of the coolest teachers at our middle school at the time. JV was undoubtedly one of Mr. TK's favorite students and because I was JV's friend, I got to meet Mr. TK. I think the first time we bonded with Mr. TK was when I told him that El Che Guevara was one of the leaders I had always looked up to. Mr. TK was all about "El Che." He really knew the history of the United States and beyond these borders. Many times, he would even wear a shirt with Che Guevara on it. Again, our middle school had or still has one of the best teachers that welcomed us, the newcomers, and wanted the best for us. Of course, not all of them were so great. There were some teachers that I had during this time that taught me what racist discrimination could feel like. Some teachers would have favorites and they were *all* white students. Like the music teacher, Mr. AR. I would ask him to teach me how to play the drums almost every day, but he never taught me. Instead, he would invite the white kids to play the drums each and every time they asked. He preferred to have a group of the white kids play the drums than give me a chance at something that would become one of my passions. The Latine kids were getting written up in his class left and right for the smallest things, but the white kids' behavior even when extremely distracting and disrespectful was passed off as no big deal. The clear difference in which he treated his students was strange and glaring.

The second semester of the school year, my dad returned to the United States. This time to stay with the family and to support us. After two and a half years, most of the family was reunited. My oldest brother decided to stay in El Salvador after he graduated with his bachelor's in mechanical engineering and later got married. For my dad, it was time for him to join his family. He contributed emotionally so much to our success here and he has been our pillar in our family ever since. The eighth-grade year brought with it drastic change, but I now felt like I finally had balance and the support to adapt to this new environment.

Running Cross Country:

I can run fast. As an eighth grader, I never really thought about how fast or how talented I was, but I was fortunate. From a biological perspective, I had enough fast twitch muscle cells to be fast and be a sprinter and I also had enough slow twitch muscles to run for longer distances. KM convinced JV and me to run cross country. Can you guess who opposed the idea of us running to represent our school? I bet you did not get it this time! It was our after-school program. For a third year we were enrolled in the after-school program, but we started to find it less and less helpful. If anything, it felt like JV, and I were missing out from doing other things at school because of it. We joined the team regardless of their opposition and at some point, they accepted that we were still committed to attending the program.

KM was super excited about us joining. The races were by grade, so he thought that we would dominate the running scene. Although cross country for middle school was quite different from high school, the purpose at the end was still to run for a distance as fast as you could. We also met NA and MH for the first time. NA was a sixth grader and MH was an eighth grader. NA was an extraordinarily talented runner from the very beginning. Every time he would run with us, we always expected that he would get tired, but this was a kid that did not know pain or exhaustion. MH on the other hand had always done Cross Country and he had the passion for running. Although he was not the fastest kid, you could tell he always had fun and enjoyed the sport.

The first race was at a private school near the area. This race was the worst I had ever run. I remember thinking to myself, what am I doing here? Everyone looked so strong and like they had proper training and preparation for the run. Our coach really sucked. We had no structure to our workouts, and we had never once warmed up or cooled down at a single practice. He would take us for a run around the neighborhood, but that was not enough to make us a formidable team. With the little training that we did have, KM and I did fairly well.

The last race of the season was at the civic center and there was a kid that KM told me was fast. This kid, JL, had been his competition throughout middle school, so he warned me about him. The race began and KM and I were leading the race against JL. Ours was a very different race in comparison to the rest of the people who were behind us. Running as fast as we could with the phrase in our mind that MH's father told us, "*Pónganle la galleta*," as a way of saying do your best. As we were getting closer to the finish line, JL started to pull away alongside another kid. KM chased them, but my body could not keep up with all of them. JL won the race, KM got third place and I finished in sixth. Such a challenging and exhausting race. All I could think was, why didn't I run cross country earlier? The season ended. I was glad to have found something I loved. JV also did well. We were starting to find a new world of opportunities.

Turkey Race:

Close to the date of Thanksgiving, they had put a flyer for the Turkey Race at our school. It was a race where the winner would take home a whole turkey! I was not really interested in running it, but KM, of course, convinced me. Cross country season had already ended, but we both were still in rather good shape.

It was a Friday. A cloudy day. It had rained so much that I thought the race might get canceled due to the slick ground. About half of the eighth-grade class had built suspense to see who was going to be the winner, KM or me. KM's girlfriend during that time had asked me to let him win so she would get the winning turkey, but to be honest my competitiveness was peaking, and I would not let anyone beat me at this race.

Mr. LE, our P.E. teacher, gathered the group of runners. The weather was cold, and I saw my breath swirl and then disappear into the cold air quickly being replaced with nerves and adrenaline. Everyone made a line, and the count began! "3, 2, 1, GO," yelled Mr. LE! The stampede of runners started. Many slipped in

the mud, making me lose balance. Others jumped high and avoided the human obstacles of students. "Damn! KM is in front of me," I said to myself right behind him. It was a race of 800 meters. Two laps around the *fútbol* field. WA, another kid from our class passed KM, but at the turn he slid in the mud. KM was again in the lead, and the rest of the runners were about 50 meters behind us once we hit the 300-meter mark. I stayed relaxed and right behind KM. I saw his pace beginning to look fatigued as we neared the 600-meter mark and soon enough I made a move to get myself in front of him. I felt in control of the race. I saw him slowing down more as I continued running. I was about 10 meters in front of him. I heard louder steps as we started to get closer to the finish line. The louder the steps got, the faster I started running and at some point, it felt like we were going at the same speed. 100 meters left to go, I sprinted to the finish line and was victorious. I defeated KM at the 800-meter mark. Maybe my perfect running distance. It was such a close and intense race, most of the people said that KM was catching up but that it was too late as I started to increase in speed.

I had won the race! Many of my peers congratulated me, including KM. It was the mutual respect that we always had for each other because the competition was beautiful. It was healthy and fun! What was funny was that I threw up afterwards, badly. I was feeling so sick that WA had to carry me back to class! JV grabbed my backpack and helped me to get to the classroom safely. I was cold, I was weak, but I felt so alive! It was a great Friday where I brought back a turkey for Thanksgiving. When I told my mom, she could not believe it! Although she had already bought a turkey for Thanksgiving, we froze the winning bird to eat on Christmas. I hope that in the future, I get to race again against KM in a turkey race.

Champions of Track and Field:

Spring of 2009 had arrived, and this meant track season. Speed trials began and were the first time I encountered real competition for sprints. There were four of us that were the fastest students from the school; KM, WT, HT and me. There was something about this team that felt powerful and like we were going to be the champions that year. During the race trials

WT and I were at the same speed. Sometimes we would tie, sometimes he would beat me and sometimes I would be faster than him. Again, it was a respectful thing, we knew that one was not better than the other one. It was very difficult to determine the faster runner.

It was the finals for the county middle schools. It was a hot day at the track of a local community college, and the team was unnecessarily stressed that WT couldn't leave class meaning we would all be late. His English teacher ignored the early dismissal.

When we arrived at the meet, we made it just in time to warm up and the 4x100 race was starting soon, the first event to begin the entire meet. We were the underdogs. It is true! Our middle school was not on the map at all. They had submitted a time for us, but we really did not know if we could run that fast. The other schools had more of a presence on track, so we showed up to the finals with most people doubting us. We practiced handoffs for the first time at the track and it was difficult to get used to it because of the track's curve. The order was HT, me, KM and WT as anchors. Compared to the other schools, we *looked* like underdogs. I was wearing an old pair of running shoes without a sole, which did not help to make matters any better.

When the time came, everyone went to their position. We had our marks, and the stadium went completely quiet. Not a single person was speaking as the referee provided the directives, "On your marks, get set," and then the gun went off! HT began with a strong start, explosive and getting ahead of some of the runners, my hand off with him was right on point and I took off at max speed for the next 100 meters! I remember hearing spectators impressed with our team's speed as I passed the baton to KM. I didn't even realize that when KM began to sprint, he was already ahead of everyone by almost 50 meters! KM then passed it to WT, and he ran leaving everyone in dust at a distance of almost 70 meters to make up in order to catch him. When I saw WT cross the finish line, I knew we had won the race. The distance that we won was incredible. Along the sideline, parents looked at us with mouths wide open in

disbelief. There was a small detail though, when WT was getting closer to the finish line, he slowed down a bit. You know it was like Usain Bolt. He would frequently run and slow down at the end of the race. WT cared more about the fact that we had already won and not so much about the time. Well, of course we won, but we were less than a second away from breaking the county's record for the 4x100 meter relay. If WT had not slowed down toward the end, we would have won the record as well. That day we won for our middle school.

We got a trophy and medals for our first-place win. That trophy is still at our middle school! It remains with many other ones that past and current generations won in running. It was a moment of euphoria winning that race. A moment of glory. I will never get tired of looking at that trophy. It was teamwork, the A Team. We were the fastest kids in the county! It has been one of my favorite races as a sprinter.

School, City, and State Recognition:

Eighth grade was a year where all my hard work that I put into my studies paid off not only in the classroom, but on the track, something I could have never dreamed of achieving. An outside organization that was partnering with the county schools would host a ceremony to recognize two students from each school. I do not think these students needed to be newcomers, but they would be the most outstanding students in the school. ZL and I got nominated and became the two recipients for this recognition. To give you a bit of background about ZL, she was an outstanding student and very cool. Someone disciplined and incredibly smart. She started with Mrs. JZ's class, but in eighth grade she began Advance ELD and quickly afterward she got out of ELD. She was in advanced ELD for only about four months. She was an adaptive learner. I wonder if it was challenging when she went to regular classes.

The assistant principal interviewed me so that she could introduce me to everyone at the awards ceremony. I have not told you this, but I hope you find this fact about me funny and maybe a bit motivating. Do you remember all the times I did not know how to speak English? I mentioned to you that my cousin was one of my first tutors, but there was something else that taught me English. When I was in El Salvador, I would watch a lot of the cartoon, SpongeBob. It has always been one of my favorite cartoons. My memory game I think is pretty strong. I was able to memorize many episodes from SpongeBob because of just how much I watched that show. My cousin was also a SpongeBob fan, and he even had the VHS to watch the show's episodes whenever he wanted. Because I had memorized the episodes in Spanish, when I watched them in English, I knew exactly what it was saying in Spanish. I didn't need the translated subtitles or dubbing, so I just enjoyed watching the show, not minding that it was in English. SpongeBob helped me with my English. SpongeBob was my second tutor.

I told the assistant principal that this was key to my learning. One of the reasons why I was able to get out of ELD so quickly. She laughed at me because she could not believe it, but she was happy that it was part of my support and success at our middle school.

The ceremony date quickly approached, and I got home early from school. I had the privilege that both my mom and my dad came to this important ceremony. Do you know what this meant for my mom? It meant no work on a Friday and no pay. It did not matter though because this was too important for her to miss. We had a good lunch offered at the ceremony and then we proceeded with the awards ceremony and the introductions of each student. The assistant principal did an amazing job at incorporating SpongeBob. The superintendent from the district schools congratulated me and I was awarded a bunch of folders and a plaque. It was funny because I had no idea of what the folders had. My attention was on the plaque.

After the ceremony ended and all awards were provided, we took a couple pictures, ZL and I, school staff and families. On the ride back home, I started to go through each of the folders. I realized that I had gotten not just a plaque, but recognition from the city and the Senate and the House of Representatives from California. The coolest thing though was that I had gotten recognition from a private university in California. They wrote me a letter and had provided me with a one-time scholarship for $2,000 to pursue an education at their campus. This was my first scholarship and if anything, I felt closer to getting used to the idea that I had only four years before I would go to college. A tear or two rolled down my mom's cheeks, my dad was driving so I could not see his face quite as well, but I could tell that he too was extremely proud of me. They both told me to continue working hard and that doors would open.

Eighth Grade Graduation:

This was one of my favorite days of my life. I wish my entire family would have been there to see me, but at least I had my dad and my aunt attend my eighth-grade graduation. At this point, I thought to myself that all my work during middle school

175

paid off. Prior to graduation day, I had been nominated for multiple awards and recognized for awards that were provided to me in the past. JV also got nominated in specific departments for his dedication to his studies. If I remember correctly, he had a nomination for History and English.

I had prepared for this day with my mom. I had the privilege of being one of the main speakers and delivering a motivational speech for my class as we looked forward to the next adventure, high school. One of my tutors from the after-school program, JW, supported me mentally to prepare for my speech. I had told him that I was nervous and that I also wanted to say more than what I was limited to. He had advised me to not read my speech and just freestyle it by saying whatever I wanted to say. I told him that I would think about it. I always wondered what it would have been to just freestyle this speech. Anyway, I think the crafting that I did with my mom produced a great result. I still have the handwritten original copy with me and the one I translated from English to Spanish.

On the day of graduation, it was a very clear and sunny day welcoming in the summer before high school. By midday, the temperature had reached at least 85 degrees Fahrenheit. It felt like the fires of hell. Everyone was burning and sweating at a local baseball field where the ceremony was held. Before the start of graduation, I was hanging out with JV and other friends. Parents took the opportunity to snap pictures of us. My dad later arrived as well as my aunt, and the students soon started to form a line to enter the field.

During the ceremony, everything started with speeches being delivered by the principal and staff. Then we had a total of six students who gave speeches, me being one of them. ZL also gave a speech as part of the six. I went right in the middle, and it seemed like I got the attention of everyone at the perfect time. I was sweating from the heat and the nerves. There was a bit of breeze which also made it difficult for me to read my loose-leaf pages. The most important thing about my speech was that I was representing my Latine community. I gave thanks to all teachers, coaches and staff from the after-school program. My speech was in English and in Spanish because I felt that it was important to acknowledge my community. To really represent the Latine community I needed the audience to hear my speech in the language that we grew up with. I still have recordings of my speech and sometimes when I look at the hard copy again, I feel lucky to have shared these words with my fellow classmates. I was happy to be the one standing in front of everyone with ZL and representing not just my Latine community but People of Color. I ended my speech with "*¡Hasta la victoria siempre!*" The phrase that I have always loved and kept close to my heart. Can you guess who was one of the teachers who yelled the loudest? Mr. TK! He got super excited when he heard my last phrase. I was proud that I was able to give voice to all my classmates who were not white.

As the ceremony continued, I was recognized for being in Honor Roll the entire time in middle school. I was recognized for being a student scholar athlete, the first time this award was handed out! Finally, I got recognized for being the most outstanding student of the eighth-grade class. I could see pride in my Latine peers. I proved to be a disciplined student who could compete and was recognized more than even the white students, whose privilege and access put them leaps and bounds ahead of me in every academic race. I made something out of nothing. I took the opportunities and worked hard. I did well on tests, and I became an athlete who was on the champion 4x100 meter relay team. I had passion for music, and I did my best in all classes even when I struggled. I always wanted to do better, and I had.

After the ceremony, many of the teachers admitted that this was the first graduation where Latine students took the majority of the awards. It felt like it was the Oscars. My aunt and my dad were super proud and if anything, they were amazed and shocked at my accomplishments and recognitions. I do not think they really had an idea of just how much I had achieved and never expected that I was going to earn so many awards.

Since we were off from school, I later went with my dad to pick up my mom from work. It was 5PM and I could see that she was tired but excited to hear how the ceremony went. My dad told her all about it, how impressed he was by everything, how I was recognized for my hard work and about the speech. I remember seeing my mom cry from the side mirror of the car. She was so proud and told me how she wished she could have been there to see me. I think my mother realized at that point again that I was going to make this trip worth it. That migrating to the United States was the right decision. Her teary eyes showed that she was a proud mother of the "most outstanding student" from the class of 2009. I hugged my mother; I cried as well and told her not to cry and that we should be happy. She replied *"Estoy feliz. Estas son lágrimas de felicidad."* I told both of my parents that I loved them, and all these accomplishments were also for them. For our fight in this country. *"Siempre adelante."*

High School Freshman Year:

A new door. That is what freshman year felt, like entering a new door for the first time. A remarkably new feeling where you must learn a completely new system. The only difference this time was that I already had friends. It was only my second year out of ELD classes, and I was meeting a lot of new people. At the same time, this was also a place that was combining students from different middle schools.

As summer was ending, we had an orientation at the high school where we got our schedules. This time I did not confuse my name like I had at the start of sixth grade. The first thing I checked was if I had any of my classes with my friends. Since I did pretty well in my eighth-grade classes, I later realized that my freshman year schedule had STEM courses, a bit more advanced than many other students. For example, I was taking Biology while most of my class was taking Physical Sciences. Another example was that I was taking Geometry and many of my classmates were taking Algebra 1. It was like a repetition of eighth

grade STEM courses. To this point, I am still questioning why many of my fellow classmates had to repeat some of these classes. What was the reason for their placement in these classes?

KM and I had very similar classes, but at different times. JV and I only had Steel Pans together, which ended up being one of my favorite classes; Mr. CS was an incredible music teacher. The year started and I had to demonstrate that I was a capable and disciplined student. The classes were so difficult at the beginning that many times I wanted to give up. It was not even Math or Science. I liked Biology a lot. I was doing okay in Geometry, but in English, I was really struggling. One of the very first assignments was to write a CLEAR paragraph. I had a nightmare understanding what a CLEAR paragraph was. If I remember correctly, I did not do very well on this first assignment.

After learning how to write a CLEAR paragraph, I had to learn how to write an essay with all CLEAR paragraphs. Ms. MG's class was something I would not look forward to at all. The books that we read were not at all interesting. I cannot even tell you which ones they were because I've forgotten them all. There was something else that made my experience in English class stressful. For most of the classes, I felt like I was on autopilot. I was doing well overall, but the devastation of my first real break up was taking its toll. I cried so much during this time.

While attending school, I also went to the after-school program I had been attending since middle school. My attendance only lasted a semester. The first semester of freshman year went by quickly. I managed to get all A's, again. I was able to succeed in English and I started to move past my breakup overtime. I made new friendships and connected with others who had always been there. Things were clicking again, and I found a group of friends that played a huge role in making high school one of my best experiences. I got closer to KM since I knew him from middle school. KM would hang out with MV who was one of the funniest friends I ever met. I had met FR, but this time was about developing a friendship and the same situation was with KY. This was the group!

Let me start by introducing you to FR. FR was actually in Mrs. BR's class from eighth grade. We would not talk too much back then, but he was a cool dude. FR is one of the people with the biggest heart. I mean the way I got close to him was because I went for lunch with all of them. As a freshman, we were not allowed to leave campus to get lunch until the second semester. I told KM that I would join them for lunch, and I met with FR first. I told FR that I would just go with them to hang out but not to get lunch because I did not have money. Do you remember that school lunch program, well that was a benefit that I had. My parents never gave me money and occasionally, I would get a dollar or two. FR on the other hand, always had a bunch of money and he was the type of person who would spend his money on others knowing that he was doing something nice for someone else.

When I told FR that I did not have money, he immediately offered to buy me lunch. I was super embarrassed but felt so impressed by his generosity and so included. I mean, he would buy lunch for many of us many times. The first lunch at a taqueria was when I knew that I had met another of my best friends. FR is one of those people that is willing to help you always without any hesitation.

I know I went further in time from freshman year, but it was important to introduce FR. Prior to hanging out with this group, winter break for the holidays arrived and it was basketball season. I had always wanted to play basketball since I was above average in my height. In El Salvador, basketball was one of my favorite sports and I was decent. My family used to play all the time. I tried joining the basketball team and I only made it to the first practice. I was miserable on the court and quite a horrible basketball
player as it turned out. Maybe it was that I was still recovering from the breakup or that my height didn't translate into the skillset I thought it might, but I decided to just focus on school. JV and KM did join the team and they ended up loving the sport.

They got really good and towards the end of the season, they were playing large amounts of the game.

Basketball season overlapped with track and field for the first two weeks. We had discussed with JV and KM that we would do track as well, and we even convinced FR to try it. FR wanted to get faster for *fútbol* tryouts the next year. Track season meant that everything was about to change, and spring was getting closer. It was time to show my speed again!

Sprinter and Varsity as a Freshman:

The after-school program was in the past now. I was still in the program, but I had asked for permission to run track. At this point, they felt it was better for JV and me to do sports. I was not really attending the program aside from some events now and then.

February arrived with rain, but I was ready to get back on track. My feet were desperate to race people. I didn't even have running shoes, but I somehow felt ready to race. I was running in casual shoes which made my feet hurt. At first, I got used shoes that were donated by other student athletes. It was the only thing I could afford at the time, and I never really paid attention to how messed up the shoes were. I was just excited to be able to run again.

During my first practices, there was unbridled electricity in my feet. I was not in good shape yet, but I was still fast. Sprint time trials for sprinters started and it was there that I really showed my speed. I was starting the season faster than everyone else. JV and KM made it right on time since the basketball season was ending. They were both in really good shape and JV had significantly improved his speed since he was on both the *fútbol* and basketball teams. I mean, he had an explosive start. All three of us were fast coming in as freshmen and this, of course, got the attention of the coaches. We were new talents and committed.

In March, the first race was coming up. The coach was so invested in our success that he offered to buy me and JV shoes. He had insisted previously that we needed running shoes and that we could not be running with vans or casual shoes. We needed *running shoes*! I was very straight forward and told him that I would use the old ones because my parents could not afford to buy me shoes. I hated asking my parents for things. My mom was limited with expenses so a new pair of running shoes were out of the question. Coach JJ took me and JV to get new shoes and pairs of spikes! It was on Saturday when we met him at a local running shoe store. This was an opportunity for both of us and we took it.

When the first race arrived, JV and I were on varsity for the 100 meters, 200 meters, and the 4x100 meters relay. This was a huge deal! We were the only two freshmen on varsity, and although we lost a lot of our races, we did pretty well for our first season. After, Coach JJ found us a sprinter coach. He was tough with his workouts. I mean many of us threw up numerous times. That was the season I also got hurt with shin splints. They did not last long, but they were part of the acclimation process of running with my new pair of running shoes.

Although I had made it to varsity, many invitational races had competitions only for freshmen and sophomores, and since I was a freshman, I would qualify to compete at this level. I did not win a lot during this year and over time, I discovered that I was better suited for the 400 meters. I actually had a very good time of 53 seconds and that is when I impressed everyone, including myself. There was one race that JM, KM, JV and I were extremely excited for. It was a frosh/soph invitational. Do you know what this meant? Medals! I signed up with JV for the 100 meters and the 4x400 meters relay. Since it was Spring, we started swimming during Physical Education (P.E.) and of course on this day of the race, I had P.E. right before my early dismissal for the race. My dad had offered to take me to the race, and we gave a ride to JV, KM and FR.

On this day during P.E., my teacher's decisions would be another jarring reminder of a lesson on racism in United States schools. My P.E. teacher was Mr. HS. The typical cocky white guy. He put a lot of effort into coming off as a strict teacher, but in doing so he would treat Latine students differently than his white students. There was a disgusted tone he would take on every time he addressed any one of us. Mr. HS's disregard for me meant that I would be waterlogged for my important race.

Before starting class, I reminded him that I had a track meet and that we had early dismissal in order to arrive on time. We would need to leave 15 minutes after the class began. I also told him that I preferred not to swim on that day because I wanted to conserve as much energy as I could before the race. He told me he wanted me to get in the pool anyways, yes, even if it was only less than five minutes of actual pool time. I got in the pool for those five minutes and then I had to get out because of the race. I guarantee you that if I had been white, he would not have made me get in the pool. Not just guarantee, but my point would be proven when *his* athletes had a game, most of them white. Not a single one of his athletes did a single minute of physical activity for class. Small decisions those in authority make can often have large impacts on those around them.

This definitely affected my mental state as I prepared before the race. I was furious that I had to get in the water and felt disrespected and tired. When I got to the race and competed, my 100-meter race went extremely well. I won in my heart, but I was not fast enough to win all the races. We waited until the last race of the day and the team changed at the last minute. JM would not run with us and instead JL would run. He had more experience with the 4x400 meters as this was his event.

The race began with me starting as the first leg. I ran under the lights of the stadium as everyone cheered for their teams. I was not really sure what my place was since every runner had a gap. Maybe when the race started, we were in second place or maybe in first. KM took the second leg and kept us in the top three teams. The third leg was taken by JV. He really kicked into some kind of turbo-speed because he was able to pass the second-place runner, but the first-place runner still seemed extremely far from everyone. Lastly, JL, the anchor leg of our relay, started to gain on the distance between first place and himself. I am not exactly sure what time JL ran, but it was one of the highest adrenaline races he ran. In the last 100 meters, I stopped paying attention to the race since I thought we would not be able to catch first place but guess what! JL never gave up and he passed first place with a difference of less than two meters. Maybe the anchor of the other team gave up, maybe it was fatigue or maybe he got confident. All I know from everyone is that JL lifted his hands because he had won the 4x400 meter relay. We were champions for the frosh/soph invitational race, and this was the first medal of our high school running career. All the hard work had paid off and we had finally experienced a win.

As the season continued, I made it to the county finals to compete in the 400 meters and the 4x100 meters relay. I also made it to the North Coast Section meet as a freshman for the 4x100 meters relay race. It was hosted at another high school from the county, so the drive there was not bad. For freshmen to be at this level, we knew that it was a start of many accomplishments and a good four years of track and running. I will always be grateful for the shoes and the spikes that Coach JJ got me and JV. He opened the possibility of new dreams. I was a runner.

Sophomore Year:

I got to sophomore year! No longer a freshman and now knowing how the high school system worked. I did not feel like a *"pollo comprado"* anymore. Many things happened this year. Do you remember that I joined track? Running became essential to my life. I stopped attending the after-school program altogether as I no longer found value in it. I had heard that if you were extremely good at sports, colleges would recruit you and provide you with a full ride, but of course the details are much more complicated, which at that time I did not understand. Since I was a sprinter, when sophomore year began, I found myself trying to decide if I would choose cross country, football from the U.S. or *fútbol* for my fall sport. I tried each sport by attending one of their practices. I could have been a good wide receiver since I had the speed. The problem was that I was too skinny to play U.S football. I went to *fútbol*, but the team for junior varsity was full of players better than me and I was not the best at handling the ball with my feet despite my love and skills. I practiced back in the Central Valley with my friends at the apartment building. I ended up choosing cross country. The track coach had told me that the fastest 400-meter runner in the county had done cross country. I thought this would be a terrific way to get in shape and stay in shape for my track and field season.

I do not regret choosing cross country. It was also my second time running longer distances. I never really thought that I would be able to do it, but it really challenged me mentally and physically. I ended up enjoying cross country quite a lot. Although I did not make it to the top seven runners for our school's team, I did win the county championship with them. This team was so amazing that they went on to win the State Championship. Do you know who was part of this? KM and JM. They became strong runners and supported the team to win state for the first time in the history of our high school! Our high school also became the first one in our county to win the State Championship. I mean, it was a huge deal.

In the classroom, my English was definitely improving. KM and I had the same classes except advisory and physical education. He actually talked to his counselor to change his schedule to the same classes that I had. KM had always been a super intelligent student but hadn't always put in 100% of his effort. Something clicked for KM during sophomore year. As we were running cross country, he saw that most of the student athletes were very disciplined with academics. KM wanted the same and since he had the same courses as me, it became as much of a competition in academics as it was on the track.

My teachers were amazing. My English teacher for sophomore year was Mr. SB. He was a teacher that would challenge and motivate you to love English. He got me to love reading. He expanded our imagination and helped us to think critically. Finally, I was enjoying English! I was also in Steel Pans! It was Mr. CS who gave me the opportunity to gain experience of playing the drums and percussion. If I have not mentioned this, I love music and percussion instruments. Mr. CS really believed in my musicality, and he supported me until I graduated high school. In freshman year, I was the most improved student in his class and in sophomore year I earned the title of most outstanding from his class. Although I did not know how to read music — you do not need to know how to read music to play steel pans — I made music with what I felt.

I had Mr. CP for Chemistry. I dominated this class! I loved chemistry, although at the beginning it was confusing. I struggled with the first assignments, but soon became the student with the highest-class grade. I had Mr. AC for Spanish! This was a fun class because it was Spanish for Spanish speakers. This was an important class. Mr. AC was also from El Salvador, so we had an immediate connection. He was strict but proved funny at times. Taking this class made me connect back to the language that raised me. After all this time, I had put so much effort into learning English, and trust me, if you do not practice a language, you will quickly start forgetting it. My mother was happy that I got to take this class for that very reason.

I had Ms. SS for Algebra 2. This class was *the* most challenging that I had during the semester. Do you remember factoring? I had a hard time with this, and it was not like I did badly in the course, but in my second semester, I earned my first B+ in high school. My grade was 89.9% and she absolutely would not round it. I was devastated. One tenth of a percentage was between me and that A, but I didn't even argue for it. KM motivated me to talk to her, but I got what I had earned. I told myself to just accept it. I really wanted to keep a 4.0 GPA, but that class grade got in the way, and I didn't fight it. This grade didn't make me any less of a disciplined student or scholar. It was just a B.

In track and field, I did great. I was a student scholar athlete, and I earned the most improved athlete in varsity that season. This season, I had also gotten much faster, something that wasn't measured by an award or plaque. During winter, I spent time with FR and KM training for track and field. I was running faster than I ever had before. I ran at the Stanford Invitational for the Distance Medley Relay with the seniors of the team, who were all state champions for cross country. That year, I also ran at the North Coast Section race, but individually for the 400-meter event, and KM, JM, JV and I became the fastest frosh/soph team to ever run the 4x400 meter relay for our high school! We even set a record at an invitational race that season. We accomplished what I could never have dreamt of accomplishing and along the way we became an extraordinarily strong group of friends who to this day I still consider to be my best friends.

You are reading about all the things that I accomplished and maybe I have made it sound too easy as I have listed many of my proudest accomplishments. Behind every award was hours and hours of hard work and pushing myself to continuously prove that I could do the things I set out to do. Unlike many of the students around me, homework took me what seemed like forever. It didn't come easily. Yes, of course I would always finish the mountain of assignments, but doing so would cost me hours of sleep daily. I would get maybe five hours of sleep each night and that was on a good day. This workload with the amount of time I spent training meant constant fatigue. This was the limiting factor to how much I would improve in the things that mattered so much to me, my running. As many workouts that were productive, there were just as many where I felt like quitting, running on max four hours of sleep. I stayed disciplined, something I knew how to do well at this point, and prioritized achievement over wellbeing for years.

Junior Year, Please No More Testing:

The third year of high school. This was the hardest year. It felt like a mile race. The third lap is always the toughest and the one that would define who the winner would be. Academically, this was probably one of the hardest years because I had to make sure to do well in all classes. I also had to do a bunch of tests because now it was college prep time. With all the dedication that I put into that year; I feel satisfied with what I was able to achieve. Even with running, huge changes awaited me, some that would make me question my commitment to the sport.

During this time, my sister started taking courses at a community college. She was working, and things were going well for her. Her schedule was stressful though because the commute was far, and she was forced to spend full days on campus with my dad. My brother had a stable job, one that was physically tiring, but of course he made it work. My mom was working with a nice family as a caregiver to their child. They were amazing to my mother and very understanding of our undocumented situation in the United States. My dad would also work sometimes. He would take care of my cousin in the afternoons. We were grateful that we had a home, family and the necessities to live.

Life is tough in the United States as an undocumented immigrant. Work never stops in order to cover the necessities, and to save money is something even harder to do with this status. You quickly learn to live paycheck to paycheck. I am sure my family could have done better with developing better habits to save money, but the know-how is something we had no access to, an invisible barrier to wealth creation and building. This knowledge is something that we need to access to build generational wealth. These skills need emphasis over the pressures of excessive consumption culture.

Let us come back to my academics. College was around the corner. This was the year to prepare and start planning for college applications. How was I going to do all of this? During that time, I did not know. I had begun to get the hang of high school, that part of the school system, I understood. But when it came to college, I was lost. I am a first generation *everything*. I am the first to migrate to this country and now it was not moving to the new country, but to an equally foreign place, college. Come on! How would my parents begin to help me with this? I am so grateful to the people who supported and guided me through the college application process. This is the kind of work that should be highly compensated. How could you compare a celebrity selling unaffordable clothes or being an influencer to someone who is a tutor and helps thousands of kids to get into college? They are the reason I got a college education at all. They paved the way making my application process much simpler, that of meeting the deadlines and following their guidance. I was extremely lucky to be at a school with these support systems and this was all due to my mom's decision all that time ago to move us out of the Central Valley and to the school districts in the Bay Area.

During junior year, I joined two organizations that supported me with my college and scholarship applications. Because of these two organizations' support, I learned about the standardized tests that we had to take for college admission. I also learned about the A-G requirements that counselors at school had not even mentioned. Counselors at our high school often proved useless and they didn't often listen to students.

You know what was the difference between the rich white kids from our school and everyone who was in the organizations that supported me with college applications? Well, the rich white kids had already signed up for the SAT and ACT their first semester in junior Year. They had tutors who would prepare them to learn how to take a standardized test. Let's be real, the SAT and ACT are tests that filter for Students of Color. These are not assessments that test for intelligence, but a test that evaluates you on how well you can take a test. You must know which questions to answer and which one you should not. When I took the SAT, they would penalize you for getting an incorrect answer by deducting points! The scoring system is not the same anymore, but during my time it was a barrier. Students of Color don't always have the resources to prepare for these tests and high school curriculums do not directly prepare you for this. Do you know another thing about these tests? They also discriminate against people for whom English is their second language. Why? Well, their questions are in English using words that are not at all common or everyday language. It is part of the discriminatory college application system that continues to hinder Students of Color.

Anyways, I took the SAT and ACT. And you know what,

despite all my hard work and achievements in school, I did horribly! I was not even average! Most of my friends did much better. At some point, I thought that I would not go to college because these tests would be the door that closed on me!

Although this was a hard year, I had classes with some of my favorite teachers. I had Mr. CP again for Physics, Mr. CS for Steel Pans. I won the most outstanding student award again for this class. I had Mr. AC for the next level of Spanish for native speakers. I had Mr. AB for English which was one of my favorite classes. The books that we read in class were some of my favorites, ones that I actually remember. His class included a lot of imagery. It was a class full of imagination and essay writing making it super fun. I remember one of my favorite assignments was to bring a song and interpret it. I also had Mr. DA for U.S. History, an amazing teacher and human being. This was a teacher that loved his job and would never get mad. Lastly, I had Mr. SN for Pre-Calculus. This was a hard class. Pre-Calculus really tripped me up at the beginning, but I was able to catch up quickly by attending his afterschool office hours to practice. Honestly, that is the only reason I did well in this class. He was a great teacher, great at explaining and at engaging, but he was an extremely hard teacher. The calculus problems were difficult. Honestly though, all the teachers that year were super chill. I could not have asked for a better combination of teachers, especially in the hardest year of high school. The best part was that KM was again in all my classes. We literally had the same schedule and that made things way easier.

This was a year where FR, JV, KM and I became really close friends. From the larger group of friends that we had, some of us decided to step away from specific situations that could have gotten us in trouble. We were focused on school, sports and college and I am glad we kept it that way. When the four of us would meet, we would always have a blast.

Cross country was great. My workouts were amazing, and I was in really good shape, but I was still always tired with my workload. This impacted me significantly in my race performance. I performed poorly which was not for lack of workouts. I was fatigued and had little sleep due to academics. I was under so much stress. I was in the top five for the majority of the season, but when the county race came, I didn't qualify for the top seven runners of our school's team. I got hurt from my knee and I straight up told Coach JJ that I was done with running. He was not happy and told me to stop making excuses. He gave me time, but soon began encouraging my friends to convince me to run again. I apologized for my actions on the day of the county race, and he later invited me to watch the team at the state race as an opportunity to find motivation again. He always believed in me, I think that is one of the reasons why he bought JV and I shoes. JV did his first year in cross country. He left *fútbol* during junior year to run. With our record and relay of the 4x400 meters, JV took it seriously and wanted to improve his time. JV had a hard time because his passion was still *fútbol*, but he made it onto the state team as the top five runners. I still remember when he passed me in the county race; He was so surprised to see me slowly ending up further and further behind him.

Track and field came quickly. We spent a lot of time training and getting ready for the season during winter. KM, JM, JV and I were in good shape. Unfortunately, in one of our workouts, JV hurt his ankle shaving weeks off his season. KM and JM were now the fastest people for distance, and we also got a new runner added to the team, NA who we knew from middle school. The reason our high school always stayed on the radar for running talent was largely due to NA. He became an incredible runner for both cross country and track and field. Junior year track started with me in the sprints. Still competing in the 400 meters, but halfway through the season, I moved up to the 800 meters. This is the hardest race in track and field, in my opinion. It takes a very specific kind of runner because you must be fast and have the endurance to finish that distance.

Every time I ran those 800 meters, I decreased my time by 1 second. At one invitational race, I was slated to compete in the 800 meters with KM, JV and others. I was so nervous because everyone had close times for that distance. There were at least two people from other schools that held faster times. This experience later became one of my college essays that opened an academic world, turning mine on its head, but we'll get to that soon enough.

Let me tell you about this race. It was a hot afternoon. The turf burnt my skin and my feet felt like they couldn't breathe. They called us to the starting line and prepared us for the countdown and familiar directives. As soon as the gun sounded, the two runners who were faster than me took the front places, taking the brunt of the wind for everyone who fell behind them. Maybe they started too fast or maybe a million other unseen factors were at play, but suddenly, I started to hear KM and JV breathing hard just behind me. The first lap was a minute and one second. I saw the opportunity. The opportunity that motivated me. Maybe it was revenge against my own aching body after missing out on the top seven before, telling myself that this would be my race. I started to make the necessary moves and slowly passed the two front runners. KM was right behind me. 200 meters to go and I took off like a jet ripping past them. I saw a burning sun with marmalade skies while the song, "*Latinoamérica*" by Calle 13 was playing in my mind. I took off and ran as hard as I could. I crossed the finish line. I came in first place. KM took second. I felt free. It was a perfect race and a new personal best. I was an 800-meter runner.

Finally, once track and field ended and having made it to the North Coast Section Meet of Champions at UC Berkeley, just two races away from state; I was nominated to participate in Boys State based on my academics. I am not sure how I was nominated, but the fact that I was, was a big deal. I had to interview for the spot and earned a place in the program. During summer I went to stay at a university to be part of this summer program for rising seniors. We were all strong students and were tasked to learn and create our own governments. My group's city project earned second place for our government design. It was a wonderful experience that we got to meet our house representatives and senators. I had earned two certificates from the California Senate and House of Representative. I must be honest that one of my favorite moments was wearing my Che Guevara shirt to the Capitol building in Sacramento.

That summer, I completed an internship at our local community clinic. This was the first time I was introduced to data as part of the healthcare system. I was able to experience the day-to-day life of a healthcare worker. I might not have realized it then, but this would have a lasting impression on me and my career in years to come. I somehow fit in another summer program for college prep. It was exciting getting to stay at CSU East Bay. Thanks to this summer program I was introduced to RV.

RV became an essential resource to me and my family regarding any immigration laws or news. Thanks to him, I heard about DACA for the first time. Because of RV, I am also here telling you my story. Junior year was hard, but I made it through, and I accomplished greater things despite things getting tougher and tougher. Now, I was almost ready to say goodbye to this high school life.

Senior Year, The Best Year:

Here is why it was the best year. This was the year that I truly got out of my comfort zone and that started academically with taking Advanced Placement courses. I couldn't really know just how difficult it was going to be until we were assigned homework before the school year had even started. What made this year beautiful was that not only did the majority of the Latine seniors become closer friends, but many of us were also taking these AP classes together.

This year was also the year that my friend's group took shape. Now looking back, I can tell you that this same group of friends has continued to be central to my life, my best friends even now. My two friend groups merged into one. I had known HG since middle school. We connected quickly and that connection never faded. He remains one of my best friends that I trust the most. KY was also in the same middle school. He's the type of person who you'll never hear making excuses. Instead, he finds solutions and is always ready to help. ER, also from middle school, was someone whom I got closer to in high school. It wasn't until one of the college prep programs that we really got to know each other. He was always the cool one who I could talk to about cars. And finally, you know EH, one of *the sixth graders,* from all that time ago. He found his way back to our coalescing group. The friend group was solid and to this day are my brothers, people who inspire me and people whom I trust.

I must admit that the first semester of senior year was difficult, to say the least. I am not sure if it was because of the classes or because we had various competitive priorities as college applications deadlines approached. The organizations that were helping me with my college applications assigned me a tutor, Mrs. AP. She would sit with me for long hours reviewing my personal statements and gathering the necessary paperwork. I submitted a total of 12 applications to colleges (four UCs, four CSUs, and four private schools). I cannot imagine how much more challenging it would have been to apply to college without her support. I would have been lost!

In 2006, all those years ago, the first college campus I visited was the University of California at Berkeley. I remember entering the Valley Life Sciences Building and seeing the tyrannosaurus rex skeleton for the first time. I was speechless. Walking through campus was like visiting a warm and welcoming little city. I could already picture myself walking to classes. I learned that Berkeley was a big deal, to say the least, and known around the world for its contributions to research and science. UC Berkeley became my dream school.

The last applications that I submitted were for the University of California campuses. My tutor and a student from UC Berkeley supported me with the application process. After clicking "submit," I already felt accomplished. All I could do then was cross my fingers and wait.

My senior year was full of hard work as my last running season commenced. Three hours of sleep became the norm with cross-country practices and races as well as the stress of it being the last year. It was the start of my last season, there was the pressure that I would never be running for this team again or any team for that matter. There was the pressure of making my times count and the moments last. It was during this time that I should be enjoying the last of everything. Soon after, I was diagnosed with a heart murmur. Though it didn't amount to much more than a little stress in the end, for a moment I thought I was not going to be able to run again. I not only had a heart murmur but a heart break at the very idea of that possibility. Schoolwork had gotten harder and harder, but what kept me grounded and disciplined was running.

We became sectional champions for cross country. We dominated, beating our competitors by 20 points! All the attention was now on us. A local newspaper interviewed us, asking us how it felt to get here and added that heading into the state race, we had a shot to win it all. The pressure of those words hung over us like a weight. We got there and it was clear that the pressure had gotten to our coach, too. He seemed to make things worse with his own stress. The State championship was a bad day. There were almost 30 schools there to compete. Having been predicted to take the title, we left that day with a lousy 10th place. The semester ended and that was the end of cross country. It wasn't quite the ending we had hoped for, but we tried. Track and field started in the blink of an eye. Again, I found myself one race away from State and running at the UC Berkeley campus, where again I couldn't help but imagine myself on the campus no longer a high school senior but a college freshman. My family was there along with my best friends. They came out to see my last official race. I had made it to the Meet of Champions, a prestigious race. Track, unlike cross country, includes all divisions combined. I was running with a wider pool of talent from D5 to D1 athletes. This race was back-to-back prelims and finals. You would race on Thursday and then again on Saturday. At that time, a day wasn't enough time to recover for me. I had never run at this level. I didn't give myself enough rest and I didn't know how to give myself the rest that this kind of event required. That day, I was fatigued. I started well enough and by the last third of the race, I was gaining on the front runners. I could hear the stands cheering me on and the familiar voices of those who had come to watch me. Those last few meters were some of the most challenging I have ever run. Maybe it was a level of training that I was lacking or maybe it was my will, but I lost. I didn't make the stand. I tell myself now that maybe I just didn't want it badly enough, maybe my time with running was up and I knew it. I ended up finishing dead last, the worst finishing position I had ever had. It wasn't so much that any of that ended up mattering. This race was special. Special because it was the end of something that had been truly important to me for so long and that the people who mattered to me were there with me to see that chapter close.

The time to hear back from colleges and scholarships had arrived. After applying for about ten different scholarships, I was also awarded one from our music department. For the third year, I also earned "Most Outstanding Student" in my Steel Pans class. I was floored when I found out I had been awarded every scholarship that I applied for. On top of that, I was accepted into all but three schools that I had applied to. The work and sleepless nights that I had put in were finally paying off.

It was the end of March. Everyone who had applied to UC Berkeley was waiting for their application results. The day arrived that the results were to be released. All day, kids were nervously talking about their acceptances and non-acceptances and the anxiety of anticipation as they logged in to see what awaited them behind the portal login screens. I waited until the end of the school day, trying not to stress or overthink every version of how things could play out when I logged into the UC Berkeley portal. I imagined what it would feel like to log in and see the "you were accepted" and the gut wrenching feeling of logging in to see the "sorry, better luck next time" message.

I headed home after practice, practically dragging my feet every step that I took to make the time go slower. I wanted to be alone when it was time to check. I went home and again let myself imagine how great it would be to be accepted into UC Berkeley. On my way home, I was positive and kept myself thinking optimistically, this could happen, this could really happen! But as I neared home, I began preparing myself for the worst. I opened the door and was alone, as I'd hoped and planned. It was 5:30PM. I turned on the computer. I logged into the portal, clicked on my application, and the next screen glowed with the message, "Congratulations you have been accepted." The letters seemed to light up the room in blue and gold. I couldn't believe what I was seeing. I quickly refreshed the computer, the equivalent of pinching yourself whilst dreaming. The message read the same. I was in the air, jumping for joy. To hell with the neighbors! The room could not contain me. With a tear or two in my eyes, I told myself that I had accomplished it. I was going to college! I would be attending the number one public school in the world.

I called my mom, but she did not answer the phone. I called JV and told him the news. He couldn't believe it! I could hear how proud of me he was in his voice. When I finally got to share the news with my mom, she was speechless and overwhelmed with so much joy. As soon as she got home, she started to cry with my dad. My parents had predicted my success and had devoted themselves to making it so. My acceptance was so much more than just my own accomplishment. It was because of my studying, discipline, and hard work, my mom's decision to move us here despite all odds, my family's efforts to survive in this country and to set us up to achieve our dreams, my friendships that supported me at school, running that reinforced my discipline to be a student scholar athlete, and my teachers from all these years and my advisors who had helped me unconditionally to the very last minute with my applications.

The next day, I found out that I was one of four students that had been accepted to UC Berkeley. I was the only Latine student that had been accepted. I felt extremely proud to be representing the resilience and beauty of this community. My hard work, migrating and adapting to this country had paid off.

Senior year was *the* year. With all that was going on, I also applied for DACA for the first time. RV, one of the extraordinary people I met during the college prep summer program at CSU East Bay supported me with the application process. It is because of him that I had the courage to apply, knowing that I was handing over my legal information and where I resided. It is terrifying to provide information about yourself to the federal agency who would now know or be reminded that you have been here without documentation. Giving information about your parents, who remain with an undocumented status, is frightening and frustrating. I think about how this protection for me inversely makes them vulnerable. DACA is unfair to my family and was a hard decision that we had to make.

I was approved with a DACA status and after a couple months my work permit arrived. It was now the second half of senior year. I took advantage of getting my license. I was 18 already and could now drive my family without the fear of getting stopped without a license or having our car taken away from us. Without the fear of getting a ticket for $500 or more. My family felt at peace knowing that I had my college path, ability to work, and ability to drive; three things that were essential to my college career.

I made it to the end of senior year. I gave a speech at my

high school graduation, as I had at my middle school graduation. I reminded my class that we were embarking on a new life where we had to take a stance on how to improve the world for us and future generations. Social justice was at the core of my message, as was the fact that we are all capable of achieving great things. Senior year was the best year.

University of California, Berkeley:

Ahh college. Do you remember your college experience? For many, college is a great experience. For others it is an experience of growth and many times of confusion. For others it is a time of stress. Well, I got to experience each of those things. Freshman year was a new start. "*Pollo comprado*" all over again. I had to learn to live with people who were not my family and how to be away from home, to take care of myself, and how to study, again.

Before I start talking about my college experience, let me tell you that I did miss my best friends from home once we embarked on our separate journeys to college. I didn't introduce you to EM during my high school journey because we became closer until college, but I can tell you that he is a humble, caring and respectful individual.

Our group of friends from home had become larger. It was going to be hard to adapt and make friends at UC Berkeley who were anything close to my best friends at home. At least that is what I thought, but I met an amazing individual during my freshman year.

One of my best friends in college, AZ, was one of the key reasons why I was able to graduate from college at all. AZ was a big support and someone trustworthy that I could talk to when things were not going well. He made me feel like I belonged at UC Berkeley.

My college experience was extremely challenging and exhausting. It took five years to get my degree. The discipline that had gotten me through high school with flying colors and awards was not cutting it at UC Berkeley. There were what seemed like unrealistic expectations and the experience felt almost inhumane. There was very little room to make errors, if at all. I was a STEM major and pre-med. Unlike other majors, STEM majors were almost always graded on a curve. Maybe it was just me, but biology, chemistry, and physics exams seemed to evaluate us on concepts that were beyond our understanding or had been hiding in between lines of the pages we read. Why we were graded in such a harsh way is beyond me. The only thing it seemed to benefit was messing with your mental health. Entry level courses were known to be especially tough. The professor's assistants made the exams, and they would make them extremely difficult to wipe out students from STEM majors. It was a matter of sink or swim.

In my first semester, I failed Chemistry 1A. I had to

retake the class and barely passed it even the second time. I failed Biology 1A, twice. Bio 1A was known as one of *the* hardest courses at UC Berkeley. My studying was inadequate for tests. It took me until junior year to get a handle on the right way to study. The number of times I cried were countless. These tests and courses reduced me to feeling stupid and incapable. For the first three years, attending my dream school became one of the lowest points in my life.

By junior year so much had changed in the political environment. The 2016 elections were coming up. It felt like the United States had fallen back 60 years. The racism and hate towards People of Color and other minority groups awoke with a violence and fury. Trump becoming president and the rhetoric that ensued took a huge toll on me. My self-esteem plummeted, I no longer found joy in what were already arduous courses, and on top of all of that, I was scared for myself, my family and friends. The talk and media coverage of what Trump planned to do, what he represented, and the ideas circulating against undocumented immigrants was too much. So much hatred aimed at undocumented immigrants permeated all parts of life at that time, it reared its head even on the UC Berkeley campus. Students from the Republican party began building walls with fake bricks along one of the most visited walks of campus. Fear started to creep in.

It felt like persecution every day. We had been reduced to

another campaign topic for both political parties. I am not exactly sure how I made it out of this whole. Maybe I never really did make it out whole, but I made it through. Again, it was the strength of my family that supported me and my great friends.

Yes, I failed some courses, but I lifted myself back up again. UC Berkeley provides undergraduate counselors and with the help of mine, we were able to figure out a path to graduate. For whoever you are reading my story, it is okay if at some point you hit a low point. It is what makes us human. Sometimes we fail, and even fail again. It happens and can happen in any aspect of life. My recommendation to you is that when you hit your lowest point, don't be scared to find help. My counselor helped me with my path to college graduation, but she also helped me with my depression during that time. She was a person whom I trusted, gave me mental health resources, and believed in me – one of the few on campus. Experiencing depression is a normal thing. It happens to us humans. Remember that you are not alone and there are people in this world who want to help you. Ask for help.

Although college was tough, I still found joy attending lectures with many scientists who were pioneers in the field. I found joy in all the friendships that I made. I found joy in the diversity in all aspects of life that this college experience provided. UC Berkeley was a time of growth and preparation for what was to come next. I knew that if I could graduate from UC Berkeley, I could achieve anything I set my mind to.

Salsa at Cal:

Salsa at Cal was culture. It was movement, exercise, and flavor! Salsa at Cal was my oasis, a way to deal with the pressure from UC Berkeley's academics and the political environment brewing around us. I took the introduction class my freshman year. When I saw DeCal, a course taught by students with the support of a faculty member, I was intrigued. I wanted to learn from the class and participate in the culture that had raised me and the music that I had grown up listening to with my family, the music that all those years ago had gotten me from plane to bus crossing bridges to standing under those tall, tall towers in San Francisco. I learned how to dance salsa, teach it, and became so invested in this group of dancers that I was soon a part of the club's board. This was my community, the thing that was missing in this place that felt so foreign. The culture of UC Berkeley was not one that I always knew how to participate in. Soon I was not only dancing but hanging out with a group of passionate people, whose friendships were a refuge from everything else. This group motivated me with my academics and gave me a place that felt safe. I was dancing, I was making friends, I was in my community again, and that felt good. Salsa at Cal will always be in my heart.

I Need a Gap Year:

I took a gap year away from Berkeley between my junior and senior year. I needed a break from academics and a different environment that would help boost my mental health and morale. I attended Berkeley City College (BCC) to complete some pre-med and major prerequisites that I had not yet completed. When I sat down in my first class at BCC, I felt at home immediately. Students at BCC were more conscious of the realities that were happening in the world outside of the bubble of UC Berkeley campus. I could relate to the experiences of many of the students. Professors seemed to care more about your success, and they would take their time teaching the curriculum. It was here that I found my joy in learning again. My confidence got the boost it needed. I was no longer failing and retaking courses. During my time at BCC, I earned a 4.0 GPA. I was able to help other students with studying habits and strengthened my own. I was back. My mental health was in a better place, I was in a better place. I was going to be able to return and graduate.

I moved back home, and I was now commuting to school. Being back home restored my connection with and support from my family. I was eating better and I was intentional about my class schedule. I prioritized exercise and made time to study and hang out with friends from home. Every day you would see me studying at a café or a library. I did not have a single day of rest until the semester finished. BCC was the reset button in my college career.

I loved my time at community college. If I were to redo my entire undergrad experience, I would have started at community college. The tuition was more affordable. I learned way more in my STEM courses at BCC than UC Berkeley. Community college can be a great start for all students.

My Last Semester as an Undergraduate:

I made it to my last semester! It was six months of sleep deprivation and studying like I never had before, but I succeeded back on the UC Berkeley campus. During my last semester, I did research in a nutritional science project and worked as a data intern.

I would from time to time teach at Salsa at Cal events and I was on top of my academics. It was probably the hardest year, but also the one that I enjoyed the most. I was able to help many of my classmates with studying for one of the hardest courses of our career, and I developed great relationships with some professors. I was juggling it all and had finally found my stride.

Then it came, the end of it all. I wrote my last paper and turned in my final exam. I closed the cover of the blue book sitting in the grand lecture hall realizing that all the years in high school dreaming of this school, all the dark times once I finally made it here, the light I finally found leaving this place and then returning, all of it was ending. I remember calling my mom as I walked back to my car and told her that I was finally done. I walked one last time through Sather Gate and told myself that I had done it, I had lived out my dream. I was a college graduate. A graduate from the number one university in the world! I was ready to share this accomplishment with my family and celebrate.

A Family Reunion:

Graduating from UC Berkeley was no ordinary celebration. It was the celebration and accomplishment of my entire family! Family came to my graduation from El Salvador and Los Angeles. My godmother who raised me during my childhood, my second mother, was making the trip to see me! I don't know how she made it happen, but she was there to see me graduate!

She arrived on May 18th. I spent the entire afternoon taking graduation pictures around campus. Around 11PM my godmother, my oldest brother and my family arrived. I walked down the stairs and as I greeted her, she stared at me for a long time trying to find the little boy she remembered in the face of the young man I had become. I immediately started crying and hugged her so hard that I felt like I was a kid once again. I grabbed her arm and wrapped it around mine and walked her to our home. She has always loved me unconditionally and it felt like nothing else to be finally reunited after 12 long years.

The night that everyone arrived was chaotic, but a good kind of chaos when family members are all over the house and there is love and warmth everywhere. My graduation was the next day! My oldest brother, who had also only just arrived from El Salvador, quickly helped us to develop the logistics of wake up and shower times. I don't know how we were able to sleep even one wink. People were in beds, on couches, and chairs. The floor was the best option to sleep. The excitement for the next day was electric in the house as we all hummed to sleep.

Graduation was again, so much chaos. My undergrad counselor came for my afternoon ceremony, my college's graduation. At the first graduation, only my family was able to make it due to limited tickets. This was the general commencement. You don't get to walk the stage, but you feel like you are a part of something big. The second graduation was much smaller and much more significant. They called my name and I walked across the stage with all my family members and friends there to be a part of that moment. A huge chunk of the audience was there for me. I had about 50 people there that day at graduation. I felt like a truly lucky person at that moment. I will never forget that day. I could finally say, again, *"Hasta la victoria siempre!"*

My First Job after College:

Networking and maintaining those relationships, especially with those who have supported you along the way, is something that isn't always explicitly taught in your college courses. Now that I had graduated, the next step was to go out and find a job. Thankfully a couple days after graduation, I had visited my teacher from senior year English, Mr. SM. He was a huge supporter of me and many of my friends from high school. During high school, he challenged me quite a lot to improve my writing, and always advised me and my friends to stay on track, not to get into trouble and to make smart decisions in college. I love visiting teachers from my old schools and catching up with them. When I talked to Mr. SM that day, I mentioned to him that I was going to start looking for jobs. I named how interested I was in working in the medical field or doing research. As it turned out, he said that his wife worked in the public health sector and offered to connect me with her to chat about my options for work.

The next day, I met with his wife in San Francisco. I arrived at the heart of Market Street. It was a jungle of skyscrapers. Her office was in a beautiful building, a couple of blocks away from the Ferry Building. This was one of the first times that I was exposed to the professional world, that of business, and work. It was new and exciting.

When I met her, we talked about job options in public health, what I liked and what I didn't. She told me about her job and the company that she worked for. After she explained her role and the mission of the company she worked for, I had more questions than answers. What exactly did her company do? How did it help the healthcare system? It ended up being a fruitful conversation ending with a tour of the office. I left our meeting excited to start applying for jobs.

When I got home, I received an email from her. She had offered me a job at her company as a project coordinator! My first job after college! I decided against starting up full time to take one last class at UC Berkeley that summer. You know what was the most shocking thing? The salary! It was much better than the data intern job and I knew this was going to help me and my family. As you can imagine, I left my data intern job. I took the last class at UC Berkeley and became a full-time employee at my first job after college. My first official job as a full-time employee! I even had benefits now. I didn't quite understand what that meant, but with time I was able to figure out why they were so important. I was fortunate to leave college and find a job in my field that I was excited about. I was in the healthcare field, my passion.

A Partner for Life:

It was a morning of blue skies and a radiant sun shining against the chrome of my motorcycle. My protection, a warm galactical suit in the heat of 88 degrees Fahrenheit. Like any romantic date, I was timid and maybe a bit too serious. I was anxious and my hands were sweating. I brought with me some extra motorcycle gear because our first date was going to be a ride along the Pacific Coast followed by a coffee and buttery, flaky pastry. On that day, I met my partner for life, GL.

GL is not the type of person that you meet every day. I consider myself extremely fortunate to be her partner. She has a beautiful smile. Her skin turns to an olive tan when the sun shines on her during the summers here. Her eyes are the color of honey. She is extremely intelligent and has a kind and caring heart. Sweet like honeydew. You know how I knew she was the one? GL has similar ideals to mine. Social justice is at both of our cores. We are both hard workers and learners for life. Although we have differences between the two of us, we understand that those differences are important in our relationship to balance ourselves. Understanding that with your partner, it is not just a huge step, but also a part of a beautiful process of growth.

Because of her, I have continued to grow in my profession. I have become the manager of data analytics at the same company that I started out in. Thanks to GL, I continue to practice my salsa dancing and my Salvadoreans traditions. Thanks to GL, I have continued to challenge myself with new goals. I continue to learn about social injustices that have negatively impacted communities of People of Color and underrepresented groups. My learning with GL feeds my hunger of wanting to do more for our communities, achieve an equitable way of life. GL has become multiple pillars of support in my life, and I am excited to continue our growth, hopefully making more of a positive difference in this world.

Where I am and Where I am Headed:

As I get ready to say goodbye to all of you, I would like to reflect. I feel content and grateful for what I have achieved. Even with all the barriers that I had as an undocumented person and that I have as a *DACAmented* person, I have tried to make the most out of every single opportunity provided to me. I have met an enormous number of people that have supported me during this journey, and I value these relationships as part of my growth in life.

I am so fortunate for my family and the sacrifices they made to come to this country for better opportunities. It has been 18 years since we left our *Pulgarcito*, and we are still here even with all the racism we have faced, the fear of deportation, and the wearisome jobs. We are still here resiliently working for a better future to have quality of life. To my parents, thank you for all your unconditional support and love that you have provided and continue to provide me with through the years. Our hard work has paid off and will continue opening more doors. To my sister, you are the strongest family member and the one that has challenged the system multiple times. Thank you for teaching me resilience and passion to continue pursuing my dreams. To my brother, thank you for all that you did when you had to step up and provide for our family and for being a listener when I needed to talk. It is your turn now to get bigger things, I know you can do it. Finally, to my older brother, thank you for visiting us, for paving the way in getting a higher education and for teaching me that quality of life is important and a priority.

I am also fortunate for my friends, teachers and mentors. To my best friends, thank you all for accepting me for who I am and for all the laughs, dancing, crying, and challenges we have faced. To my partner for life, I know things will change, but I am ready to accomplish it all by your side.

I am Jose. A *DACAmented* individual from El Salvador that migrated to this country in 2006. I am a brother, a son, a partner, a friend, a best friend, a community leader and a manager of data analytics in the healthcare field. I lead the data infrastructure for two programs based in the state of California integrating behavioral health in primary care and making healthcare equitable for People of Color in Los Angeles County. I enjoy running. I have a passion for motorcycles. I love my family, girlfriend, and my friends. I still worry about my status in this country as DACA continues to be under attack, recently being declared "illegal." I have moments of anxiety and moments of depression while I worry for my future, the future of my family, the future of my friends and the undocumented community. I will not stop fighting for the injustices that my undocumented people, People of Color and underrepresented groups face in this country. I will not stop living my life because of my legal status in this country. One day I will become a leader in the healthcare industry and continue working on making the system just and equitable for all people.

To all of you, don't become too comfortable with how this country is being run. Choose individuals who will make a change for all people and bring equity. Be an activist! Call out injustices and let your voice be heard when something is not right. Don't let politicians rob us of our futures by making a decision that you never hired them to make. Remember that they work *for* us. If you are able to vote, use that privilege to make change, remembering that your neighbor also lives in the world you are voting into existence. Those around you are impacted with how you decide to vote. Build up your social consciousness and don't be afraid to have uncomfortable dialogue with someone that might not think the same way as you. Be courageous and bring social justice to the forefront. I need your help and we need each other to make this world a better place for today and for future generations. *¡Hasta la victoria siempre!*

Erick Palafox

Salutations, Dear Reader! Your presence is deeply appreciated as you embark on this journey through my chapter among the other fascinating ones in this book. I trust this small paragraph finds you well, and that you are surrounded by happiness, health and dear friends and family. Within the following pages, I will unfold the story of my life, starting from March 1990 and reaching its culmination in January 2024. In a departure from usual bibliographic accounts/memoirs, I have chosen an unconventional approach to recount my tale. Throughout this narrative, you may encounter a mosaic of obscure references spanning history, science, and the tapestry of pop culture, including nods to video games, movies, TV series, songs, and the random musings that populate my mind. The intent behind this eclectic style is to mirror the fluidity of my thoughts, influenced by what some may deem a "bad case" of ADHD. I trust you find joy in this unorthodox journey, and I extend my heartfelt gratitude for joining me in this small but meaningful part of my life story.

"A Brown Star is Born" not ft. Lady Gaga

A higher power:

> "Do you solemnly affirm that you will tell the truth, the whole truth, and nothing but the truth?"

Luis Erick Aguirre Palafox:

"Yes. I solemnly swear that this is my story and my truth. That I can finally tell my story and someone will listen."

Once upon a time, in a galaxy far, far away, in a distant realm of Puebla, Mexico, to be precise, my tale begins. However, an intriguing twist in the cosmic narrative unfolded the day I was born, as strangely, I wasn't officially registered at birth. The reasons behind this peculiar circumstance remain shrouded in mystery, yet I suspect various contributing factors: firstly, I emerged into the world as a fragile infant, facing uncertain odds of survival. Why bother registering a child who might not endure the winter? Secondly, my biological parents, in their youthful indiscretion, foresaw my adoption by my maternal grandparents, whom I endearingly call "The Parental Units" henceforth. And lastly, the Parental Units resided in the culturally rich state of Oaxaca, a place brimming with beauty and tradition. Fear not, dear reader, for a year later, The Parental Units officially claimed me as their legal child in the colonial city of Santo Domingo Tehuantepec, Oaxaca.

Xbox sound
"ACHIEVEMENT UNLOCKED: The Parental Units aka. Rock #1"

Fun Fact #1: Apparently, I was the only male baby born that day in the hospital.

In the tapestry of my early years, I find a tapestry woven with threads of joy and warmth. Our family, nestled in the vibrant embrace of *el barrio* (the neighborhood), may not have been adorned with opulence, yet my parents, the steadfast architects of my childhood, ensured that the foundation was laid with the essentials: happiness, health, and safety. I find it akin to navigating the realms of a video game, where the metrics of Happiness, Health, and Safety shape the character I have become. In this current chapter of my life, I recognize the need to enhance these vital stats. As for my migration to the United States, the details fade into the recesses of my memory, as I was old enough to comprehend yet too young to retain every nuance. The primary motive behind our journey across borders was to open the door to enhanced educational opportunities, a quest ignited by the desire to refine my English skills. While I had been acquainted with English from 1st grade, there exists a chasm between understanding the language's rules and syntax and actively engaging in its practice. It's analogous to mastering the intricacies of flying a jetliner through a computer simulator—a far cry from the challenges of flying a huge metal machine in the real world where there are tangible consequences.

Should I stay, or should I go now?

Should I stay, or should I go now?

If I go, there will be trouble

And if I stay, it will be double

So come on and let me know

Should I stay, or should I go now?

This question lingers in the air, bearing the weight of complexities and contradictions, demanding introspection into the roots of my decision to make the United States my home. The straightforward response may be that this is where I have learned to navigate the intricacies of adulthood. Yet, the narrative behind this choice unfolds in layers, tracing the trajectory from residing in an "emerging economy" to embracing life in a "first-world country." In 2003, my family moved to Ciudad Juarez, a border city in the northern Mexican state of Chihuahua, standing in stark contrast to El Paso, Texas, just across the border. At the time Juarez, rife with crime, presented a paradoxical backdrop against El Paso's distinction as one of the safest U.S. cities. This theme of paradox and dualities would echo throughout my life. During 8th grade, I navigated the educational landscape in Mexico, while concurrently commencing high school in El Paso during my freshman and part of my sophomore year (courtesy of a peculiar detour into summer school despite stellar grades). Residing in Juarez at the time meant a daily ritual of crossing the international border bridge, a routine repeated 468 times over approximately 1.3 years. This intricate dance between two worlds required a constant code-switching of my entire being—Mexico versus the United States, a dual existence layered with background stress during my formative years at the tender age of 14-15. Talk about a transformative time.

The year 2005 brought a new life chapter as my family made the significant decision to establish roots in Santa Rosa, California. While I had visited the city before, the notion of a permanent move had never crossed my mind. The motivations behind this pivotal decision seemed intertwined with the pursuit of a better life—a perpetual quest to elevate the main stats of Happiness, Health, and Safety. Additionally, there was a subtle undercurrent pulling us closer to my biological mother, a presence in my life that had been intermittent during my formative years. The absence of my biological father, who died in 2001 without being part of my life at all, might have also factored into the choice to relocate, fostering a reconnection with the biological maternal figure who had never been a constant in my upbringing.

Embarking on my sophomore year, I found myself enrolled in a "prestigious" high school. However, the sheen of prestige did not shield me from the challenges of adapting. Surprisingly, I, who had always effortlessly forged connections with my peers, became an introvert, struggling to weave a social fabric. The nuances of teenage social dynamics pressured me to conform, urging me to suppress my native language and hide the cultural nuances of my upbringing—like the delectable bean sandwiches crafted by Parental Unit A (mom). A misguided attempt to camouflage my roots resulted in a paradoxical revelation: my peers easily discerned my outsider status, laid bare by my accent and the idiosyncrasies that marked me as an outlier in the mosaic of their normality.

"Picture it, Santa Rosa 2006!" (that was for you Golden Girls fans). 2006 was the year I first encountered discrimination, or at least the time my teenage mind first processed the act. On another ordinary school day, my high school counselor summoned me to discuss post-graduation plans. As we navigated the terrain of requisite classes for High School completion, the conversation took an unsettling detour into the realm of discrimination. I learned that California's academic standards were purportedly different from those in Texas, a proclamation delivered with a subtle elitist undertone. Confident in my academic prowess—my Texan transcripts full with A's—I proposed the subject of concurrently tackling Geometry and Algebra the following academic year to avoid extending my high school years. The counselor's response, unfiltered and delivered to a barely 16-year-old me, landed like a seismic wave: "Well, your people are not good at math." Those few words etched themselves into the canvas of my consciousness, becoming a core memory that reverberated through time, relentlessly questioning my identity for years to come. "Your people"—a classification that set me apart, signaling inequality and exclusion from their societal ranks. "Not good at math"—a stereotype wielded like a blade, further distancing me from my peers. Once more, the paradox of being a participant in society while relegated to a position of inequality was glaringly apparent.

After that incident, I reached a breaking point and decided to take matters into my own hands. I reached out to another high school in the area, opting for a private institution. It was a gamble, with potential for both high risks and rewards. Ultimately, it turned out in my favor. On the day I was scheduled to meet with the admissions people, I walked for two hours since I did not know how to get to the school by bus, and I still did not have a driver's license, as, despite being 16 years old, my circumstances prevented me from legally obtaining one.

Fun fact #2: I got my driver license at 25 years old.

Upon meeting the new high school counselor, I candidly shared my situation. Unlike the previous counselor, she granted me the opportunity to take both Geometry and Algebra simultaneously. Defying the prejudiced notion that had been imposed on me at the other high school, I excelled in both classes, proudly achieving A's. To the person who once claimed, "Your people are not good at math," I say, "Take that!" Two years later, I proudly graduated from the private high school, securing the position of the second-best student among my graduating class.

Legally Brown: Aged for 18 years

Turning eighteen shocked me. Turning eighteen usually marks the day that for many signifies celebration and the transition from childhood to adulthood. However, my eighteenth birthday was a mixture of excitement and fear. While the prospect of being recognized as an adult intrigued me, the looming reality of navigating adulthood in the United States without the protective shield of being a minor was a source of unease.

I entered adulthood during the spring semester of my senior year of high school, a time when my peers celebrated university acceptances and dreams coming true. Instead, I found myself retreating further into introversion. Although I received an offer from a private university, an unspoken intuition and force compelled me to stay close to home. In an act of self-sabotage, I chose not to pursue higher education immediately. It took years of introspection and numerous therapy sessions to unravel the intricacies of my decision. The revelation emerged: I was afraid of the unknown and the absence of stability. The only constants in my life were my Parental Units, always there for me when I needed them most. Subconsciously, I clung to the comfort of having them nearby, realizing that, amidst life's uncertainties, their unwavering presence was a solace I couldn't bear to part with.

Fun Fact #3: Although the mentioned university was just 75 miles from my parents' house, at that moment, it felt as distant to me as if it were 140 million miles away.

Fun Fact #4: 140 million miles away is the average distance between Earth and Mars.

Instead of pursuing higher education. I decided to keep working at a friend's small company nestled in the mountains between Santa Rosa and Calistoga. The origins of this chapter of my life trace back to the year 2005, precisely when I first moved to California. Stay with me Dear Reader as we take a detour and unravel the circumstances that led me to the fateful decision to work for a man that had and continues to have a profound impact in my life. As I mentioned just a few words ago, it was the summer of 2005 when this all happened. One day I decided to go to work with my older sister at a summer camp nearby. After her shift was over, we decided to pick up my older brother who also worked nearby. While he was not there, I got a chance to talk to the man who would soon become my boss. The interaction was brief yet meaningful as the usual inquiries about my identity and experiences surfaced. "You are Osmar's little brother, do you go to Carrillo? (the awful high school I previously alluded to)" "How are you liking Santa Rosa?" "How are you doing in school?" "Oh, you were working with your sister today?.... Would you like a job?" It was that final question that altered the course of my life from that very moment onward.

Xbox sound
"ACHIEVEMENT UNLOCKED: Tim Duenas aka. Rock #2"

Tim Duenas, a name that resonates through the pages of my life, transcended the mere role of a boss and transformed into a pivotal figure shaping my teenage and young adult years. Little did I know at the time that this man would impart invaluable lessons on financial responsibility, the delicate art of balancing work and life (still working on that!) and the unwavering commitment to stick to one's principles. Beyond that, Tim also took on the role of a chef, treating my coworkers and me to delicious and nutritious lunches, a gesture for which I am forever grateful (and for making me appreciate tofu). Tim also fostered and encouraged a work environment where music filled the air thanks to the countless CD's he owned and ranged from classical music to 80s rock to world music. We also had an open fridge policy, which stood as a testament to his generosity. Additionally, Tim is the person who would always ask "Mr. Erick, how are you and your family?" "Mr. Erick, can you please help me with these math problems?" "Mr. Erick, I read this on National Geographic. Do you know more about it? And if you do, I have lots of questions".

More importantly, Tim's significance in my life transcends these interactions. At a time when I struggled with the stress of assimilating to a new country and assuming a forced identity for the sake of social acceptance, Tim saw me for who I truly was. He treated me not as an outlier, but as an equal while also recognizing my potential and providing unwavering support. Though time has passed, the regret lingers for not extending an invitation to Tim for my high school graduation—something I carry as one of my deepest regrets. Yet, Dear Reader, a spoiler alert awaits: Tim attended both my Bachelor's and Master's graduations (see sections below).

Tim, the major architect of my teenage and young adult years, deserves my heartfelt gratitude for imparting unforgettable life lessons. Dear Reader, in your own narrative, I encourage you to reflect on the Tims in your life, the individuals whose influence, guidance, and genuine kindness have left an enduring imprint on your journey. And let us not underestimate the profound impact of simple gestures and conversations. Sometimes, it is the seemingly innocuous ones that can set in motion significant and life-altering events—even simple questions like "Would you like a job?"

Forever 21

Now, as you journey with me, Dear Reader, you might be wondering about the significance of these recurring "Rocks" in my story. To unravel this concept, we must delve into my community college years that mostly spanned my early 20s. Fresh out of high school and grappling with the economic recession of 2008, my initial reluctance of just keep working gave way to a visit with a counselor at Santa Rosa Community College by the end of the year. In the discussion about admissions, future steps, and course selections, I faced the uncertainty of not knowing my goals or specialization, a definite early manifestation of my undiagnosed ADHD. Opting for a pragmatic approach, I chose to take general education classes while also prioritizing work to help support my family. However, I found a natural gravitation toward the sciences, particularly Earth and Planetary sciences like Astronomy and Geology. My fascination led me to all available astronomy classes, coincidentally taught by my high school biology teacher. Although the community college offered just one geology class with a separate lab component, I discovered a profound connection to the subject that served as my grounding force. This marked the beginning of my deep dive into the captivating mysteries hidden within the geologic time. Returning to the theme of "Rocks" in my life, these Rocks transcend the geological realm; they represent the individuals who have positively impacted my life, shaped my character, and serve as pillars of stability. These people, much like the bedrock that forms part of the Earth's foundation, provide the grounding force that has shaped my identity and contributed to steadiness in my life.

As my time at community college continued, the routine remained relatively unchanged. I pursued general education classes while simultaneously navigating the demands of work. Yet, within this unaltered time of my life, another pivotal figure emerged. Dear Reader, do you recall the community college counselor? His name is Rafael Vasquez, and, as you have likely discerned from other chapters, he serves as the compelling force behind the making of this book. Rafael, to me, is an enigmatic person, shrouded in secrets and brimming with boundless wisdom. Knowledge, I have come to realize, is indeed power. Rafael has devoted significant portions of his time, energy, money and resources to the community, specially focused on aiding the Latinx and underrepresented communities. The extent of his commitment, evident in his prolonged work hours extending well into the night, remains a mystery to me. Among the wonderful friends I met through him, we would often joke that he might be a secret vampire, a notion humorously substantiated by his affinity for wearing sunglasses most of the time and the sleek black cars he often drives.

Despite these playful speculations, Rafael has left a permanent mark on countless lives. We, his "kids," constitute a family. Between us, I am his "Kid #47," marking the encounter that took place back in 2008 when I stepped into his office clueless about my life's direction and uncertain about my identity. While the exact count of his "kids" eludes me, I am confident that the number reaches into the hundreds. Beyond the numerical aspect, Rafael stands as the person who dismantled the blindfold and shattered the forced persona I had grappled with since my teenage years. Through him, I learned to cherish and take pride in my heritage—a lineage stretching back to ancestors who migrated from Aztlan to Mesoamerica, weathering the challenges brought by Spanish conquest, enduring colonialism, and surviving the tumultuous struggles of Mexican civil and political unrest in the late 20th century and much of the 21st century.

Rafael, with his unwavering commitment to helping those in need, consistently impresses me. Often, he extends his aid before individuals realize they require assistance. A truly remarkable gift. In conclusion, Rafael entered my life as a community college counselor and evolved into one of my steadfast and enduring rocks. Thus, that said:

Xbox sound

"ACHIEVEMENT UNLOCKED: Rafael Vasquez aka. Rock #3"

Fiat Lux and Fiat Meds

In the early and mid-2010s, my journey led me to the University of California (UC) Berkeley after years of navigating community college and sporadically attending classes at community college. After accumulating enough credits to transfer, I was stubbornly determined to transfer only to UC Berkeley. The magnetic pull of the university eluded precise reasoning, but perhaps it was the proximity to the San Francisco Bay or the renowned geology program with world-class scientists. Before sending my application, I made a personal pact: "I will apply only here, and if I do get accepted, so be it! If not, I'll interpret it as a sign." With the guidance of Rafael's educational counseling, bolstered by Tim's moral support, and the imminent introduction of Rock #4 (Gene Gorman), I successfully applied and got accepted to UC Berkeley. Go Bears!

Xbox sound
"ACHIEVEMENT UNLOCKED: Gene Gorman aka. Rock #4"

Fun Fact #5: I got accepted as a "German language" major but the day of orientation, I decided to talk to my coordinator and asked to attend the Geology student's orientation. Sometimes you just need to ask the universe and the universe might smile back at you!

Prior to enrolling at UC Berkeley, I lived with Gene for a substantial period in the East Bay. This marked a significant move for me, as I now found myself 55 miles away from the Parental Units, the original anchor of personal stability. Surprisingly, living with Gene felt like discovering a new home. I experienced tranquility and security, and Gene generously provided for basic needs at the time, spanning from food and school supplies to transportation costs. More crucially, Gene possesses the remarkable ability to recognize innate talents instantly, fostering and maximizing one's potential. Getting accepted into UC Berkeley would have been an even more formidable challenge without him, not only due to the basic financial stability he offered but also the emotional support and encouragement that propelled me to take the daring step toward continuing my education. It is noteworthy that the Parental Units remained oblivious to my educational pursuits beyond high school. Their inquiries focused on work and other aspects, with my occasional reminder that I was also engaged in studies at community college (or UC Berkeley, or spoiler alert: UC Davis). As I mentioned earlier, their primary concerns revolved around three key metrics: Happiness, Health, and Safety, with Education not factoring into the equation. Eventually, I ceased updating them about my academic endeavors, recognizing that their disinterest wasn't a rejection of moral support but rather a belief that university attendance was as straightforward as walking in, signing up, and attending classes. An easy endeavor seemingly accessible to anyone. There were numerous occasions when my mom would compare my university schedule to my little cousin's elementary school schedule, emphasizing their lack of understanding about the complexities of higher education. It is important to highlight that neither of the Parental Units graduated from elementary school, reflecting the challenges of growing up in rural Mexico in the 1950s. Dear Reader, I often engage in self-reflection, urging myself to "Check your privilege, Erick. Check it."

My time at UC Berkeley served as a profound reality check, exposing me to a diverse tapestry of individuals from around the globe, each carrying their unique stories and aspirations. Unexpectedly, I also formed a supportive network of friends hailing from various backgrounds, sharing long nights immersed in studying for our Mineralogy or Petrology midterms and finals. Little did I realize then, these were the initial instances of "trauma bonding" that would shape my academic journey but would forge long lasting friendships. Berkeley also marked the beginning of my foray into research, initiated by a meeting with Professor Walter Alvarez, renowned for his theory on an asteroid impact causing the extinction of non-avian dinosaurs. Walter presented me with a potential project that evolved into my Senior Honors Thesis, later becoming part of my Master's research and my inaugural publication as lead author. Prior to that, I contributed to a smaller project under Walter and a collaborator from Spain, resulting in co-authorship on a paper and my first oral presentation at a national conference as an undergraduate. Reflecting on my time at UC Berkeley and the impactful figures that shaped it, Gene's acknowledgment of my potential and unwavering support, coupled with the camaraderie of classmates and friends preserving my sanity, and Walter presenting an academic opportunity I eagerly embraced, all contributed to this transformative part of my life.

Lastly, during my short yet impactful period at Berkeley, I received a diagnosis that caught me off guard—ADHD. While it surprised me, those who knew me probably wondered how I had not noticed sooner. The diagnosis acted as a guiding beacon, shedding light on the reasons behind my idiosyncratic behaviors and interpersonal dynamics, some of which I continue to understand and navigate to this day. While the clarity it offered put many aspects of my life into perspective, the medication's tunnel vision emerged as a double-edged sword. It's almost witchcraft how a tiny pill can address chemical imbalances in the brain, making the world seem more organized and stable. However, it also fuels uncontrollable hyperfixations, ranging from tape wall art to weaving shoelaces, attempting to learn Esperanto, learning how to fly a Cessna plane via Flight Simulator, etc, etc etc. Even with medication, ADHD remains a 24/7 struggle where its influence is determined by various daily factors. To borrow a phrase from Game of Thrones, "Madness and greatness are two sides of the same coin. Every time a new Targaryen is born, the gods toss the coin in the air and the world holds its breath to see how it will land." That is me, except substitute "Every time a new Targaryen is born" for "Every time I take ADHD medication." Dear Reader, I extend my wishes for your well-being, both physically and mentally. If you find yourself facing challenges, please remember that resources are available and that caring individuals surround us. You are never truly alone.

The City by The Bay

If you're going to San Francisco
Be sure to have hella money to pay rent.
If you're going to San Francisco
You're gonna meet a lot of techies there.

Oh, San Francisco, a city that sparks love and disdain in equal measure. It's a magical realm of contrasting scenes, diverse aromas, and vibrant colors. Whether you've heard the tales or not, let me assure you (especially if you haven't experienced it yourself), the stories are 100% authentic. San Francisco, to me, is more than a city; it's my home. Defining why is a challenge—perhaps it's the organized chaos of a metropolis, the myriad scents both delightful and not-so-pleasant, or maybe it's the eclectic mix of people, rich history, cultural mixture, and breathtaking landscapes. Can one truly claim to be a San Franciscan without a beloved hole-in-the-wall Mexican (or insert your preferred cuisine) joint that may or may not risk a bout of food poisoning? Jokes and genuine stories aside, San Francisco is a place where I can unequivocally declare, "I belong here."

Fun Fact #6: I dislike when people say "SF" to refer to the City and County of San Francisco. I pay too much rent for an outsider to be lazy and not pronounce the whole name.

San Francisco marked the arrival of Rock #5 in my life – Scott Carpenter. Our worlds seemed poles apart initially, yet little did we know, our paths would intertwine, leading to transformative changes for both of us. Much like the streets and walls of San Francisco, Scott became a witness to the peaks and valleys of my life from that moment on. Beyond being a mere observer, he stood and still stands by my side, always offering support in countless ways. Scott imparted countless valuable lessons, but perhaps one of the most pivotal being the importance of occasionally indulging oneself, reassuring that I am also deserving of material joys without feeling the weight and guilt of the world on my shoulder. While we might disagree on 70% of superficial matters, this fades in comparison to our alignment on fundamental values such as family and personal happiness. Defining our deep connection and kind of relationship has always been challenging, a struggle that seems to span ages. Yet, from our earliest encounters, it became clear that Scott would play a profound and enduring role in my life. From my perspective, I can encapsulate it with this brief statement: "Scott is one of my Rocks."

Xbox sound

"ACHIEVEMENT UNLOCKED: Scott Carpenter aka. Rock #5"

A Tale of Two Flat Cities Part I: Davis, CA

Embarking on my PhD journey led me through the corridors of two distinguished universities: The University of California Davis and the University of Kansas. Following the completion of my Masters at UC Berkeley, I continued working at the Berkeley Geochronology Center, where fate intertwined my path with a PhD student from UC Davis. Engaged in similar techniques for dating the geological record, he not only shared his experiences but also encouraged me to explore opportunities at UC Davis, prompting a meeting with his advisor. A year later, I found myself at UC Davis, navigating the uncertainties that accompany relocation to a comparatively smaller city. Yet, my primary concern was not the city's size but the potential disturbance to the stability provided by my Rocks – my support network. Despite the initial apprehension, I reminded myself of my own advice: "Take risks and do not be afraid." So, after settling in Davis, my first act was to locate the nearest Mexican restaurant. Spoiler alert: The experience left me slightly disappointed as I never found one.

Fun Fact #7: During the initial months, the only method that could lull me into sleep was playing a 10-hour YouTube video featuring "city noises." The tranquility of Davis's streets, though appreciated by some, felt unnerving and "unnatural" to me, lacking the constant hum of cars, ambulances, and airplanes flying overhead that I was accustomed to.

Embarking on my first quarter in Davis during the fall of 2019 was initially filled with excitement and the typical pondering of "I have no idea of what I am doing." However, the landscape drastically shifted on March 11th, 2020, as I celebrated my 30th birthday and simultaneously found myself teaching a geology laboratory. On that day, an email from the Dean confirmed our collective suspicions: the school was closing its doors due to the escalating Coronavirus pandemic. Dear Reader, whenever you come across this memoir, be it in a distant future or as a contemporary witness of 2020, the subsequent 2.5 years were marked by uncertainty for numerous individuals, myself included. I fully understand I was by no means the most affected person out there, to say that the Coronavirus derailed my PhD journey would be an understatement. Though I could detail the direct impacts of the pandemic on my life, I'd prefer to leave this challenging period behind.

In Davis, I was fortunate to weave profound friendships, primarily with my PhD cohort and fellow graduate students in the Geology department. These connections evolved into a robust support system, a lifeline that proved invaluable when life threw its inevitable curveballs (beyond the challenges posed by the pandemic). Having companions who shared the same stress and uncertainties inherent in PhD programs was remarkably comforting. We sailed together into the uncharted waters of science, collectively navigating through unknown realms or occasionally sinking into their depths. The camaraderie forged in these moments of triumph and struggle, a kind of trauma bonding, sustained our journey. These friends, my invaluable "Pebbles," served as the MVPs of my Davis life, preserving my sanity when my Rocks were distant. On another note, I must acknowledge the other anchor that kept me grounded and sane in Davis: my cat Keroberos, affectionately known as Kero. In times of darkness and turmoil, Keroberos was a constant source of solace, ready to cuddle on the bed or the couch, emitting the soothing purr that, as they say, has the power to alleviate emotions and minor pains. Thank you, Keroberos, for always purring for me.

CONTENT WARNING: The following paragraph contains discussions of self-destructive behaviors and emotional distress.

Despite the myriad of meaningful connections I forged in Davis, honesty compels me to admit that an undercurrent of resentment towards Davis also flows within me. It was within the confines of this seemingly tranquil town that I encountered both the ephemeral warmth of "love" and the chilling specter of self-destruction, not once but twice. Maneuvering through the already arduous landscape of a stressful PhD was compounded when returning home meant facing the aftermath of a partner's distressing actions, including daily attempts to "self-delete." Or confronting their daily reliance on alcohol to "forget and get numb" while simultaneously expecting you to get in the car with them (which I never did when such extremes occurred). The toll of witnessing such pain and coping mechanisms from people you love took a toll, casting a dark shadow over my academic pursuits, social connections, and my soul itself. Despite the availability of resources, the limitations imposed by the pandemic rendered assistance challenging. Moreover, attempting to assist individuals who rejected help exacerbated the situation. Even now as I engage in therapy and rely on prescribed medications to navigate the aftermath, the specter of PTSD lingers. The echo of a train horn or a sudden bang against a wall triggers visceral anxiety, reminding me that the brain has an enduring memory. Remarkably, physical locations also harbor recollections, and every return to Davis, despite its serene exterior, resurrects a fragment of anguish within me, a poignant reminder of the struggles endured in that city.

Yet, Dear Reader, much like Sour Patch Kid candy, let's shift the mood from something sour to something sweet. Let's take a sharp turn and delve into my favorite holiday of all time: Christmas Eve.

'Twas the night before Christmas, when all through the house,
All the creatures were stirring, cuz' it's a Mexican house'

Undoubtedly, the most treasured time of the year for me is Christmas Eve. It's the day when our family's traditions and the memories of a distant homeland come to life once more. Christmas Eve serves as a portal to a bygone era, a time when we can reclaim our old selves and revisit the customs we've cherished for decades. As the years have passed, Christmas Eve has undeniably evolved. The days of our extended family traveling to gather at my great-grandmother's house are now distant memories, faded like old photographs. However, without fail, each passing Christmas Eve whisks me back in time, as though I'm reliving every one of those cherished evenings from the past. My memories and senses converge into a singular experience, making it feel as if each year is my very first Christmas Eve. It's a paradoxical sensation, where the past and present seamlessly meld, and I find myself both grounded in tradition and propelled into the future with hope and anticipation. Christmas Eve is a time capsule of joy, nostalgia, and the enduring bonds of family, reminding me of the beauty of our ever-evolving traditions and the constancy of love across space and time.

Los Cinco Sentidos – The Five Senses

In the tapestry of my memories, Christmas Eve holds a special place—a magical, enchanting night that engages all five of my senses and weaves together a rich blend of personal and shared family experiences.

El Olfato - Smell

The very air seems to come alive with the aroma of a freshly cooked Christmas Eve dinner, infused with the richness of tradition and the warmth of cherished memories. It transports me back to the vibrant markets of Mexico, where the tantalizing scent of street food dances through the bustling streets. Yet, amidst the culinary delights, there's a distinctive scent that lingers in my recollections—the unmistakable aroma of burning gunpowder from the cheap fireworks and other "cuetes" (small fireworks). It's a scent deeply etched into the fabric of my soul, and to this day, I can conjure it, on command, in my mind. Whenever a similar scent reaches my nose, whether from fireworks during the 4th of July or New Year's Eve or a distant bonfire, an overwhelming feeling of coziness and warmth envelops me. It's a soothing sensation, a potent smell that, as a child, probably fried some of my odor receptors, but paradoxically left an indelible mark of comfort and nostalgia.

El Gusto - Taste

The memories of my family's Christmas Eve dinners are filled with the exquisite taste of traditional Mexican dishes passed down through generations. Tamales, tacos, mole, and dulce de leche, each meticulously prepared, bring a symphony of flavors to my palate, and with every bite, I feel a deep connection to our cultural roots. However, in the days of yore, the crowning glory of our Christmas Eve feast was a seafood masterpiece. One cannot reminisce about Christmas Eve without conjuring images of our family's unique version of the "turducken," but with a maritime twist—crab inside fish inside another fish combined in a tantalizing creation. The fact that we never gave a name to that delectable monstrosity, which would have made even Frankenstein's creator blush, fills me with a sense of regret. So, what shall we call it? "Mariscrabbado?" "Pescangrejo?" "Pescrejo?" The possibilities are as boundless as the joy and laughter that echoed through our holiday celebrations. Yet, as I reminisce about my childhood, I realize that the feasts may not have been as extravagant as I recall. It is all relative and bigger when one is a small child. The joy, unity, and second servings, however, were always abundant. Our Christmas Eve gatherings were a time of togetherness, where stories of past celebrations were shared, and laughter echoed through the room.

El Oído - Hearing

The room would come alive with the joyous symphony
of laughter and animated conversations as our extended family
gathered, creating an atmosphere that resonated with the vibrant
fiestas of our Mexican heritage. Amidst the revelry, my father's
tales held a special place in our hearts. He would share stories of
his daring adventures as a young fisherman, all while confessing
his lack of swimming skills. We'd listen in awe as he recounted
the time he ran away from home for being physically and
mentally mistreated, finding refuge in an abandoned boat
christened "La Perla." As he continued, the narrative took us
back to his teenage years when, due to necessity, he and his
friends embarked on adventurous river swims, sometimes
punctuated by heart-pounding encounters with sharks, stories that
always elicited gasps when he would mention friends getting
eaten occasionally. Classic family Christmas stories.

Amidst the lively gatherings of our extended family,
another cherished auditory element of our Christmas Eve
celebrations was the festive music that would blast from the old
stereos scattered throughout the house. As we indulged in Dad's
adventurous tales and enjoyed the warmth of togetherness, the
merry melodies of Christmas carols filled the air. The room

would resonate with the joyful notes, and even my father's anecdotes seemed to gain an extra layer of magic when accompanied by the cheerful tunes. What made it even more endearing was the realization that beyond the walls of our home, other families were crafting their own Christmas memories. Sometimes, when I stepped outside to stargaze with the cousins or play with "cuetes", I could hear the distant echoes of different stereos belting out the same beloved Christmas songs. It was a funny and heartwarming reminder that the spirit of Christmas transcended our own family's celebrations, uniting us with others in a shared tradition of joy and festive music. In those moments, the world felt just a little smaller, and the bonds of family and community became all the more evident.

Even as a young padawan, I was aware that the party seldom ceased before the break of dawn. There were those moments when I'd awaken in the dead of night, greeted by the comforting sounds of my family's merriment, a testament to the enduring bonds of kinship. These memories remain etched in my heart, a cherished tapestry of our shared stories and the timeless joy of our gatherings.

La Vista - Sight

Sitting by the twinkling Christmas tree, the soft, warm glow of the lights enveloped me, evoking memories of the luminarias that often line the streets during the holiday season. But amidst the tranquility of those luminous moments, there were other aspects of our Christmas Eve celebrations that added layers of magic and complexity.

The nights were often punctuated by the brilliant light of "cuetes," the fireworks that painted the sky with vivid colors, filling our hearts with wonder and excitement. And then there was the family reunion, the sight of close and distant relatives we'd see once a year, coming together from near and far to share in the joy of the season. The little ones would gather around the television, captivated by the Christmas movies and shows that entertained and enthralled us, our wide-eyed wonder proof of our innocence amplified by the enchantment of the holidays. And, of course, there was the sight of family drama, the humorous and sometimes tumultuous interactions that we'd all laugh about later, a reminder that even amidst the most cherished traditions, life's imperfections added a unique and endearing quality to our gatherings.

El Tacto - Touch

The warmth of my family's embrace and the playful tussles with my cousins always transported me back to the heartwarming embrace of close-knit family ties. Our night was also often punctuated by the physical manifestation of family friends. Those moments were a testament to the deep sense of belonging that permeated our gatherings, a feeling that transcended the boundaries of blood and emphasized the bonds of love and togetherness, both mentally and physically.

As a good Mexican family, we exchanged thoughtful gifts beneath the shimmering Christmas tree Christmas day morning, not Christmas Eve night. The excitement of unwrapping each package never failed to ignite my sense of wonder. The anticipation, the laughter, and the shared moments of happiness as we shred the wrapping paper like little gremlins to reveal the hidden treasures delivered by a magical white intruder never ceases to put a smile on my face. These exchanges were a reminder that the true spirit of the season was found not only in the gifts themselves but in the love and appreciation we shared with one another.

A Tale of Two Flat Cities Part II: Lawrence, KS

My PhD journey also led me to the Sunflower State, primarily because I was co-advised by another professor at the University of Kansas in Lawrence. Initial impressions of Lawrence defied my expectations; it struck me as a blend of Berkeley and an older East Coast city, like Boston. Although similar in size and population to Davis, Lawrence possessed a distinct character. I experienced less culture shock than anticipated during my regular visits, occurring at least twice a year and, on one occasion, extending to a six-month stay. Lawrence emerged as one of the most "liberal" medium-sized cities in the Midwest, adorned with downtown buildings proudly displaying LGBT+ flags and "Black Lives Matter" signs on windows and doors—a pleasant surprise given my initial encounters in small towns along the KS-MO state border. Those early experiences, marked by unsettling stares at gas stations, highlighted the challenges one might face as a DACA recipient and other underrepresented communities. Dear Reader, each return to Kansas or the Midwest prompts a careful reassessment of my privilege. More importantly, in Lawrence I forged connections with more of my "Pebbles" and encountered my latest "Rock" in my life, Mary Kaiser.

Xbox sound
"ACHIEVEMENT UNLOCKED: Mary Kaiser aka. Rock #6"

It might not always be evident in my narrative, but it does not take long for me to sense the people who will become one of my Rocks and will play a pivotal role in my life. Mary was no exception. Introduced by my wonderful Kansas friends Matt and Michael, my instant connection with Mary was undeniable. She radiates love and positivity, truly lighting up the room. From Mary, I learned to ease up on myself, especially during the challenging years of my PhD in Davis, which, as you already know, were not the best. Those years left me feeling sour and extinguished some of the fire within me. Mary helped me rediscover my true self and connect with my emotions—a challenging feat for someone with ADHD. Perhaps the quick bond with Mary was facilitated by our shared experience with ADHD. Sometimes, having someone who fully understands an aspect of your life that others might not is the key to forging deep connections. ADHD bonding, akin to trauma bonding, is indeed a real and powerful thing.

The more I reflect on it, it seems like I'm gathering Infinity Stones for my own personal Infinity Gauntlet (a nod to Marvel Comics and/or Marvel Cinematic Universe fans), each symbolizing a fundamental aspect or value that defines who I am.

Rock #1: Unconditional love and persistence

Rock #2: Kindness and endless curiosity

Rock #3: Love for my heritage

Rock #4: Raw potential and determination

Rock #5: Self-love and awareness

Rock #6: Emotional healing

Endless gratitude to my Rocks. You shape the person I am today, and I genuinely recognize that, even if it sounds like a cliché, I cannot live without you.

This is the End… Hold your breath and count to ten

As I type down these words, I hold onto the hope that when you read this, the situation for DACA recipients has taken a turn for the better. I aspire that we stand on equal ground with those born in the United States. Personally, once I reach that point, be prepared, for I am determined to instigate change in OUR society. My mission is to ensure that future generations, facing similar challenges or resembling a little brown star like me, understand that they can overcome. But if you are in similar circumstances, please know that YOU ARE NOT alone, that there are always people willing to help. Discover those individuals, your personal Rocks, who provide stability in your life and assist you in optimizing your individual Main Stats, whether they encompass Happiness, Health, Safety, Education, Love, and more. Lastly, always keep in mind that words—be they written, spoken, or unspoken—possess no authority to define who you are or limit your potential.

I express my gratitude to you, my patient and understanding Dear Reader, for accompanying me through the narrative of my life and allowing me to share my truth. To that end, allow me to share a poem that deeply resonates with me:

"Do not go gentle into that good night,
Old age should burn and rave at close of day;
Rage, rage against the dying of the light.

Though wise men at their end know dark is right,
Because their words had forked no lightning they
Do not go gentle into that good night.

Good men, come on it the last wave by, crying how bright
Their frail deeds might have danced in a green bay,
Rage, rage against the dying of the light.

Wild men who caught and sang the sun in flight,
And learn, too late, they grieved it on its way,
Do not go gentle into that good night.

Grave men, near death, who see with blinding sight
Blind eyes could blaze like meteors and be gay,
Rage, rage against the dying of the light.

And you, my father, there on that sad height,
Curse me, bless me, now with your fierce tears, I pray.
Do not go gentle into that good night.
Rage, rage against the dying of the light."

-Dylan Thomas (1914-1953)

XOXO,

Luis Erick Aguirre Palafox

(Top left: Rock #1 aka the Parental Units opening Christmas presents. Top right: Parental Unit A (Mom) and I at the Chinese buffet. Bottom: Christmas portrait with the older brother, Parental Unit B (Dad) and a cousin,)

(Tim Duenas (Rock #2), myself and my coworker Kassi working
for Tim circa 2010)

(Holding for dear life (I am afraid of heights) onto Rafael Vázquez Guzmán (Rock #3) while visiting the top of the 220 ft tall Monumento a la Revolución in Mexico City)

(Left: Gene Gorman (Rock #4) and I being cool cats during a winery tour in Calistoga, CA. Right: Selfie with Gene, Abbey and Tim Duenas (Rock #2)

(My many adventures with Scott Carpenter (Rock #5): At The Killers (my favorite music band) concert, top left. Typical summer in the rocky and foggy California coast, top right. On a boat in the middle of the San Francisco Bay watching the Blue Angels airshow, bottom left. In Death Valley National Park (my favorite park), bottom right.)

(Mary Kaiser (Rock #6) and Scott Carpenter (Rock #5) taking a selfie. I could not be there with them due to PhD commitments)

Maria Salcido

¿Me valoran aquí?

I believe that every immigrant who comes to the U.S. should, at some point, educate themselves on the country's history. Understanding how this country came to be and how it gained its wealth better helps us understand how we got to where we are now. There is no denying the U.S. was established on usurped land that indigenous people have inhabited since time immemorial. Indigenous people were pushed off their land through a series of broken treaties, corrupt deals, waged wars, forced migration, reservations, and genocide, amongst other practices of settler colonization, and with more and more land acquired, the young empire's European settlers turned to the old practice of slavery to obtain its wealth. However, the kind of slavery practiced in the U.S. would turn into something never before seen: chattel slavery based on a racial system. Chattel slavery is the practice of treating the enslaved person as an object, property, or something less than human. In chattel slavery, the condition of being enslaved is passed down to your children. In the U.S., this created a vicious cycle of generational enslavement for Africans and their descendants, African Americans. Though a combination of enslaved African labor and indentured European servitude made up some of the exploited labor during the British rule of the 13 colonies, chattel slavery would become the primary source of wealth for the young country. Now, you might wonder, "What does this have to do with immigrants?". Have you ever heard the phrase "immigrants built this country"? That phrase excludes the fact that the foundation of the U.S. was built on the stolen land, the resources of Native Americans, and the forced labor of enslaved Black Americans. Until we, as immigrants, can agree on that, we will continue to see this country through a distorted lens. One that seeks to separate us from building community with our Black and Native relatives because when we fight amongst ourselves, the system grows more robust. However, our strength is unmatched when we create meaningful bonds within our communities and across Black, Indigenous, and Communities of Color.

This country is divided partially because we cannot agree on the creation story of the U.S. In some classrooms and homes across the U.S., people are taught that this country was founded on ideals of liberty and justice for all. This may have been true for the founding fathers, who were white, wealthy, institutionally educated men who owned land. These ideals were not readily applied to most people in the country. Additionally, under this version of the story, the acts of Native American genocide, multigenerational enslavement of Black Americans, and corruption are played down. In turn, an idealistic version of this country is told that has brought masses of people to migrate to this country with the hope of a better future. That is to fulfill their version of the American Dream. It is important to note that inspiring people, impactful ideas, and revolutionary practices have been created in this country, mainly by the systematically disenfranchised members of this society. However, it becomes hard to truly celebrate the victories when we are not honest about the raw truths of how this country came to be one of the most powerful on earth by exploiting the masses to benefit the few. Until we come to a common understanding of this country's true origin story, we are destined to continue living in a divided and stagnant state making the same mistakes as previous generations.

I was born in Culiacan Sinaloa in the mid 90's. The first five years of my life were spent in a mountainous area in Sinaloa. Unfortunately, I don't remember what it was like to live in Mexico. Some of my favorite stories are those told by my family when we gather after eating a home cooked meal, and a story breaks out about our life back in El Rancho. I ask as many questions as possible to better understand who we were as a family before coming to this country. My earliest memories are of me crossing the border. I can recall the fluffy coconut-coated pink and white marshmallow cookies with a delicious strawberry filling flavored center on top of a firm yet tender cookie we ate during one of our rests. I also remember drinking water from a gallon of water with a mountain as the logo with a plastic white strap (Crystal Geyser). Every once in a while, I walk by those cookies or gallons of water at a store, and it reminds me of how far I've come. I also recall coming across an area where we were instructed to leave the only belongings we had brought behind. My mom refused to throw our only belongings into the lake of clothing and other materials left behind by previous people making their way to El Norte. There was a couple amongst the people who were making the treacherous journey with us. The kind man helped alleviate my mom by helping carry me on his back. I often think about that couple. I don't know what would have happened if their sense of community and humanity hadn't been present to help us that day, especially as the coyote and other people would have seemed so far ahead of us at some points. I don't know their name, and I don't know where they are, but I hope that their kindness has been paid back tenfold.

I grew up in this country, and my family, friends, and community are here. All of my memories and experiences, whether good or bad, are from this country. The more I learn about the people who have fought to hold the country accountable to its principles, the more I am inspired that there can be a sense of unity in making this country a place that takes accountability for its past and seeks to create a better future for all, not just the powerful. Yes, I know this is idealistic, but moments of unity have brought about change in this country. Many of those moments continue to be led by the most vulnerable people in this country. Though those moments of change have been thwarted by the interests of the wealthy and powerful, change can happen again. However, that change will always be under threat, especially if there is no sense of community and accountability toward maintaining the change. Whatever we people in this country seek to change will be easily coerced, especially when we don't see each other's humanity. When we can understand and appreciate our differences and choose to come together despite them, there can be a concerted effort to bring about change for the future of this country and the world.

I always knew I was undocumented. My parents never made me feel as though I needed to be ashamed of who I was or where I came from. I have always been proud of being Sinaloense. Though Sinaloense slang and style have become more popular amongst other Mexicans in recent years, after the glorification of narco culture through telenovelas and mainstream interpretations of corridos, being Sinaloense in Northern California in the early 2000s was totally different. Whenever my siblings and I mentioned we were from Sinaloa, we were typically met with associations to el narcotrafico. I even had some friends whose families were cautious at first when finding out that my family was Sinaloense. When introducing myself, I have had to navigate people's limited perspective on the drug trade in my state. Though el narcotrafico and organized crime have caused a lot of violence across Sinaloa and various states in Mexico, at the core of these hotspots of the drug trade, there are human beings. People who are trying to make a living and survive in a system that is corrupt and puts profit over human lives. Some have been in this lifestyle for generations, and the conditions of cartels running their area have become a norm.

In a broader sense, I grew up Mexican in a working-class household. My family settled down in a white middle-class area. If my memory doesn't fail me, the first non-white teacher I had was in community college. I began learning about Mexico's history before colonization and in community college. That is where my sense of pride in being from Mexico grew more profound, as did my self-knowledge. Though history was my favorite subject in school, I always felt something was missing. Especially when it was time to learn about Black, Indigenous, or People of Color. The history book only had one page (if you were lucky) covering the non-white historical figures.

In grade school, I went through the motions of trying to get good enough grades and staying out of trouble. I never really questioned why we came to this country; I just assumed it was to "live a better life", as I would hear my parents say this to remind us to stay on a straight path. It wasn't until I was a teenager that I asked my parents why we came to this country. I was surprised to hear that we were fleeing from violence. In high school, I was a student-athlete and involved in a club for Latino students. I didn't really have an idea of what I wanted to do once I graduated. I was introduced to the idea of going to college through my best friend. Who, at the time, had two of her older sisters in college, and she was going to follow in their footsteps. My older brother had been working since he was a teenager and didn't attend high school. My older sister had graduated high school and continued working. I participated in a college registration informational hosted in the library. Rafael V. encouraged many of us Mexican and Central American students to apply to the junior college to further our education. Little did I know that close to 10 years later, I would be teaching social studies through an ethnic studies lens in a high school in South Central Los Angeles to predominantly Mexican, Central American, and Black students.

I transferred from my local community college to UCLA with the support of my family, friends, and greater community. Me puse las pilas, and I took up to 21 units one semester to rack up enough credits and prerequisites to transfer to a four-year year. After graduating with my associate's degree from community college, I became the first person in my family to obtain a college degree. Since then, I have become a double bruin, obtaining my bachelor's and Master's degrees from the University of Los Angeles, California. My understanding of my positionality as an immigrant in this country has been thanks to the Mexican, Central American, Black American, and Indigenous professors and students I have had the privilege to learn with and from. In college, I understood how crucial it is to know who you are and the history of your people. Especially stories told about us by us, not through the eyes of outsiders. Being exposed to our stories and accounts of events through the eyes of communities of color and other marginalized groups helps mend generations of biased stories told inside and outside the classrooms.

The older I get, the more I think about returning to Mexico. The thought of it creates a mix of emotions that often leave me in the same place, the unknown. This country is my home; it's taken me a while to claim it, but it is my home. It is where I have lived for the majority of my life. All of my schooling has been here, from Kindergarten to Grad school. I have made all my friends in this country and fallen in and out of love here. I have all the memories with my family and friends in this country. My job experience ranges from working at Burger King as a cashier to a high school social studies educator. Though I love Mexico dearly, I do not know it like I do this country. I only know Mexico through stories. The stories that my family tells when we gather around the table after a meal, and something sparks up a conversation of the past. I feel a duty to keep those memories alive and pass them down to my future children and grandchildren. However, I would like with all my heart to have memories of my own to recant of my motherland. Yet, I don't remember Mexico at all. At a certain point, I realized I often avoid looking up pictures because they present me with the harsh reality that I cannot return freely if I go.

My youngest sister recently went to the place we left behind in the mountains of Sinaloa over two decades ago. It was a huge deal for the family. She returned with gifts for us and stories of her experience of our mother country. It was a delight for me to see her go to Mexico and return with many positive experiences. When she was there, it almost felt like a part of me traveled with her when I saw her social media posts. I was especially overjoyed to hear that she really liked Mexico and that the place where I grew up for the first five years was beautiful. At the same time, I couldn't help but feel impotence. Why can't I just go… Why not just leave? Will I have a future in this country when these politicians continue to use us, undocumented immigrants, as scapegoats for their political games? Do I continue to build my life here? Do I want to go into my 30s, still in limbo, as a pawn in someone's game? Will things be different if I move to Mexico? Will they be the same? Am I romanticizing a place I don't remember? I don't know.

What I do know is that I am a product of a beautiful culture and a loving and badass family. I am surrounded by supportive friends, and I have tried to maximize my potential in this country, much like many other undocumented immigrants do every day. We should not have to be perfect or even exceptional to obtain a pathway to citizenship. Though this country can make you feel disposable, I want to remind you that we are humans, we are members of a community, and we have our families, whether blood or the one we create along the way. Our experiences, hopes, dreams, and aspirations matter; even if we decide to leave, our time spent here was not in vain. We matter outside this country just as much as we do within it. If I can leave you with anything, it would be to learn about your own history.

Then, look up the history of resistance to colonial systems by marginalized groups in this country and across the world. Maintain hope that there will be a better future for disenfranchised people and take action consistently and intentionally for that future to come to fruition, even if that means you might not get to experience that future.

Perla Sandoval

I was born in 1993 in a rural place in Mexico. I have a younger sister as well as an older sister. I grew up learning how to milk a cow to *echar abono* (add soil) in the corn fields. My parents taught me and my sister to love *el campo* (rural life) as well as work hard at a very young age. My parents were from *el campo* and grew fruit, vegetables and raised chickens. One of the best memories of my life is the childhood memories I have when I used to live in Mexico. I won't change anything about my life there as a kid. My father started crossing the border to this country in the early 1990s to work in the fields of Fresno, California and the Central Valley, along with his father and brothers. My mom was a typical Mexican woman in our town that was often left alone in Mexico raising her children while her husband worked in the US for a year or more and then came back to visit us.

It wasn't until I was 12 that my mom decided she wanted me and my sisters to have a better life in the US and insisted my father bring my family to the US. My father had been unfaithful to my mom and already had a son in California and my mom didn't want my dad to "forget" about his family in Mexico, and decided to *aguantarse* her anger towards my dad's infidelity to make sure me and my sister had a better life in the US. My mom taught that if she didn't pressure my father to bring us over while, one day when older we were going to live a very hard life in Mexico and wouldn't have a bright future or much opportunities in life. She knew what she was saying because a lot of woman that I grew up with as kids are alone in Mexico raising their kids while their husbands are in the US working, while some of them were left alone because their men came to the US and haven't gone back in years or others came to the US with their kids but its been hard to live here without an education and getting used to this culture.

(My parents, my older sister and me, Mexico 1994)

My mom had to leave her family behind and come to the US to a man that had been unfaithful to her, she wanted to come so bad not for her but for her three girls, for me and my sisters to have a better life and have an education and have a bright future with a lot of opportunities. When I came to the US It was very clear to me why I was here in the US, also my mom would often repeat to us, *que le echaramos ganas en la escuela y que nos portaramos bien* (to do well in school and behave). My mom and dad had also told me and my sisters that we were only coming to the US for 5 years and then we were going to go back to Mexico, it was kind of a mixed message because they had said we were coming to have better opportunities and a better life, I never actually thought we were going to ever go back especially after going through a lot to come here. I crossed the border with my mom and sisters in 2005. It took us long days and it was one of the scariest things I had and have experienced in my entire life. Being surrounded by many people while trying to cross, going from stranger's house to house not knowing what to expect and being away from my mom for days, me and my older sisters were all on our own. To this day I still remembered two things, one that the last *coyote* (smuggler) that crossed me and my sister over to the US, told me to not tell anyone the way we were smuggled to the US and two that my father used to tell me to not tell anyone at school that I didn't have papers and if anyone asked where I was born to say I was born in LA.

I got to Los Angeles, California and that was the first time I saw a big city, so many people that looked very diverse. That day I got to my godmother's house and we knew of two murders that happened in the block. One was a black man that had been shot while me and my godmother's kids were playing in the gated driveway. That night there was another one where a Latino man had murdered his girlfriend three doors down my godmother's house. I was scared to see all this was happening and my mom and younger sister hadn't crossed the border. I was already missing everything I had left behind in Mexico, my home and my dog, Valto, I had left in Mexico. The US seemed very scary for me, someone that lived in a ranch where there were only about ten homes spread out, a church and a small school. Days later my mom and sister were able to cross the border and arrived at my godmother's house in East LA. My father and my older sister and I were waiting for this to happen so we could move to Merced, California where we were going to live and go to school. My father lived in Marin County where he had now been working as a house painter for some years.

I went to seventh grade at a local K-8 school where it was a difficult and scary process to adjust to school. Some of the challenges that I faced were to learn English and understand the culture I was living in. Many of the kids at my school were Latinx but were not as shy and timid as I was and I worried that I turned like them and my mother wouldn't approve of me. My parents, especially my mother, liked me and my sisters to be quiet well-behaved children. My job was to do well in school, behave and make my mother proud. I felt like she had made such a sacrifice to bring us to this country that I felt a lot of pressure to be an excellent kid in her eyes. Many times not knowing English made me feel less than others and also affected my self-esteem, I remember this science class where the teacher and her aid treated me and other language learners like little kids by the way they treated us, they will not allow is to have a lot of autonomy or saw us as trouble makers that they had to constantly watch and talk to without respect. Unfortunately, I was not the only one that had a hard time at my first school in this country, one day my mom also experienced it when she came to the school office. My younger sister that was in 2nd grade was being bullied by some kids in school where she didn't want to go to school and my mom came to the office hoping to find a way to speak with her teacher when a lady in the office spoke English to my mom and was yelling at her when she spoke to the lady in Spanish. This was the last time my mom tried to talk to someone at our school.

It broke my heat to know that someone at my school, the place that I tried so hard to do well and hope to be treated with respect and feel that I belonged one day was the place where my mom had been greatly disrespected. Now that I am old and can understand many things at my age, I wonder how in reality my mom felt like sending us to school, to the place where she told us we need to listen to our teachers and *portarnos bien* (behave) and not cause problems wits other kids. Did she really felt we were free from mistreatment, misunderstanding or discrimination at school because we were kids and we were in the United State where people do things right and follow the law? I still don't know how she may have felt, this is something I haven't talked to her about and do hope to one day ask her.

My mother, my sisters and I lived in Merced for about a year and a half when later my mom asked my father if we could move to Marin County where my dad was currently living and working. My older sister, who at the time was a sophomore in high school started hanging out with friends that smoked marijuana and were gang members. My sister was coming home smelling like mariguana and my mother was worried she was using or could soon be using other substances. My mom, being worried that *iva a perder a su hija* decided that it was best we moved where my father was. All this time was hard for me as well because I was starting to get used to my new ELD (English Language Development) teacher, Mrs. Ayala, a Salvadorian English teacher that was very nice to us and where I felt I was starting to finally learn English and how the US life worked. I felt a big responsibility everytime my mom was worried or upset at my older sister's behavior. I felt like I had to make up for it and not ever talk back to her and be rebellious and instead be the kid she wasn't disappointed in. To this day I haven't ever told her that growing up I was always trying my very best to not disappoint her like at times she used to say my sister was. As I write this, I hope my sister never felt she was a disappointment to my mother, although I don't think that is true. My older sister has had her own traumas and has had to heal many wounds. She became a teen mom in high school and experienced domestic abuse (that as a result allowed her to get a U Visa) from her partner and today she is a successful young woman who has her own business and earns 3 times more than I do. I went to college and got a Masters degree and she never attended college. Growing up I always looked up to her and I still do.

Living in the Central Valley of California I was going to a school that was predominantly latinx and many of them their parents were migrant workers who worked in agriculture. My mom once applied to work in the fields and through her interest in working in the field, I was able to qualify to be part of the Migrant Education program. This program helped me and my family access services and resources. Through it, I was getting more help in class from a lady from the program that helped me and other migrant students. My mom also had regular visits and meetings facilitated by the program. I remember getting a bag of school supplies from them that made me so happy. Up until not long ago I still kept that bag at my mom's house. The Migrant Education program helped my mom also start English classes in the afternoons, it was a great program for my family when we first got to the US and were lost.

(First week after arrived to the US, March 2005)

Many things, however, changed when I moved to Marin County in 2006. The school that I went to was predominantly white and all teachers were white. There was a nice lady from Ecuador that helped me and other latinx students in class and during after school tutoring. She was a very nice lady that let me and other students have lunch in her office. At this school, I experienced a lot of social anxiety, I was very lost in school and there were times I didn't want to go to school. It was hard for me to talk to people and get out of "my shell", like people would say. I never refused to go to school or pretend to be sick because I knew that I wouldn't be doing my part of *luchando* (keep forward) in this county, also I didn't want to disappoint my mother or give her any trouble so I managed to finish school there. Now that I am writing my story, I really see how many sacrifices my family and I have gone through while living in this country. I adapt to a new culture and language in many ways. One was definitely, trying my very best to copy what the white kids did and behaved like in school. I started picking up an accent that at times people wouldn't think I also spoke English. I also tried to dress in colors and styles similar to white girls. I felt a need to connect and fit in. It was hard for me to dress like I used to dress back in Merced. I never wanted to change my skin color, hair or eyes but definitely the way I spoke and dressed. I didn't know I was actually doing this until later while I went to college and took an ethnic studies class in Sonoma State University that I was asked to think about ways I've had to adapt to the main white culture while living in this country. I guess I hadn't really given much thought to it before until I took this class in college. I am glad that growing up my mom demanded that we spoke Spanish at home and that we were only to speak English at school. I think this was a good idea because if not I would have lost in a way a very important aspect of my identity. Now that I work in school, I see a lot of Latinx students that have lost their Spanish and it seems like in my humble opinion losing an important aspect of their identity.

After being in the US for about a year and a half, I wanted to really go back to Mexico. I was missing my life there a lot. I would be crying a lot secretly. I know I was not the only one, my mom that had left everything behind was with no doubt going through a lot of pain herself. Soon after we came to the US my mom's mom had gotten really sick and two years after she passed away. The fact that I knew all the sacrifices she went through made me stronger for her. My sisters were struggling a lot to adjust to school, we all went through a lot together but to this day we haven't really talked much about our struggles. I think that is sad. We just continued through life and have tried to make the best out of it. I really admire the immigrant community that leaves everything behind to live a new life in a new country hoping to have a better life and more opportunities.

I have now lived 18 years in this country and I still remember my life in my ranchito life if it was yesterday. One of the things I remember is how kind people there are, people will help one another and watch out for one another like family. I also remember the days I used to go fishing with my father to a big lake near our home and would return home right when the sunset was approaching. I also missed how I used to live in front of my school, a school where most of the students were my cousins and there were only 17 kids at out school. I also miss Saturday's where we would wake up in the morning to walk about an hour to my grandparents and some Saturdays I wanted to wake up extra early to watch my grandpa milk his cow and offer to help him. I also remembered gathering my cousins and going with them and my uncle to a mountain to get leña (fire wood). I also remember the days that I used to shower in the creeks after a nice day of long raing. I also remember the days I used to go mushroom picking with my mom and sisters. These are the days I greatly miss and as I write this of course I can't help but cry.

Some days have passed since I wrote my story, part of me wanted to not say more but deep inside I felt like you needed to hear it and it was important. Living in the US has been an interesting experience. A long time ago I realized that I wasn't going back to Mexico. I wasn't here for 5 years but for the rest of my life. That was my reality and eventually I made peace with that.

After high school I went to college but before I was able to get there several things happened that made it hard and almost discouraged me from attending. After managing to go to middle school and later high school I wanted to go to college. During my freshman year I was taking some sheltered classes where all of the students were English learners. While I was in school I had a hard time relating and talking to my white counterpart as I was taking regular classes that I barely understood anything in. Throughout high school I was pretty much lost. I failed math 2 years and failed the CAHSEE twice. The CAHSEE was a California Exit Exam that people had to take in order to graduate from high school. Students had three opportunities to pass it to be able to graduate. Taking the CAHSEE was very hard and I felt it impossible to pass it because the reading comprehension, writing and math were areas that I struggled with a lot.

Focusing and understanding was very hard for me and it still is, I always felt that I had to work three times harder than my peers in order to barely do okay. Several times it crossed my mind that I may have a learning disability, this didn't come to me until after when I was in college, I learned that this was a thing for people. During my junior and senior year specifically students in my class talk about college and where they had applied. I remember listening to them and feeling bad because I knew I wanted to do that after high school but it didn't seem attainable. I hadn't learned anything about colleges around my house or the process to go to college. My counselor did come to one of my classes and explained something about deadlines but listening more about it was frustrating because I felt lost. I wasn't getting how it all worked and all seemed impossible.

A month or two before finishing high school, for the first time I went up to a lady that sometimes helped Latinx students and knew some Spanish she learned in Spain. I went to her office and asked her if she could help me apply to College of Marin, my local community college and she told me that she didn't know. This was very discouraging for me to hear because part of me didn't believe her and instead felt like she didn't want to help me. I knew she had a son that was also a senior at my school and he was going to college. Hearing that "No I don't know" was very discouraging. I didn't know who else to ask as not very many people spoke Spanish in my school.

I only saw my counselor once a year at most, to talk about my schedule and she didn't speak Spanish.

One day months before graduation there was this person that started to come once a week to one of my classes and talk to us about our values and culture. This was the first time someone came and talked to us about this and I really started trusting her. This person held a PhD in education and spoke Spanish. She was the person that helped me enroll into college a week before my graduation. She drove me and a few other students to college to start an application. It was thanks to her help that I enrolled into college.

She might have told me more about how college worked and financial aid. I didn't really know so I started to pay out of pocket for the first year. This person worked for a local organization and her area was working with youth in schools. I came to her office every Saturday and did volunteer work. After sometime she promised me that she was going to pay me as I was staying with her for most of the day. She asked me to write the date and hours I come in. She later quit her job and she never mentioned or told me about getting paid. This is something that to this day my mom doesn't forget and tells me that she took advantage of me. I have mixed feelings about it as she was the only person that did help me get to college and I feel like if it wasn't for her I wouldn't have known. I didn't know the names of my local community colleges.

Not having documents was hard growing up as I didn't think I could do many things like be able to go to college, get help to finish college or even work. Many times I thought my opportunities were limited because on top of not knowing English I was also undocumented. I felt scared to tell anyone that I didn't have papers as my father and mother have warned me and my sisters to never talk to anyone about that.

After community college I went to Sonoma State University and got a Bachelor's Degree in Psychology after that I went to San Francisco State University and got a Master's Degree in Counseling. I have worked as a counselor for 3 years. The reason why I wanted to be a school counselor is because I wish I would be there for students like me that need someone that speaks Spanish and can relate to them. My family is very proud of my accomplishments and my niece, now 13 years old, admired me as she knows I have gotten this far not knowing English and being undocumented. If I am able to inspire her, I am more than satisfied.

In conclusion, after writing a snap of my life, I think that it hasn't been easy but I never gave up. I appreciate my mother for always being there for me. This is one of the most important things I always tell myself every time I feel like something is hard and seems impossible. I remind myself of the hard things I have endured in life and I overcame because I never gave up. Even if you don't have documents it's important to know that there is nothing impossible and you can accomplish many things. There are kind hearted people out there that will be there to help you if you need help, you just have to be brave and ask for help.

Thank you for taking your time to read part of my life. I don't really talk much about me so you got to know a lot about me.

(My sisters and I during my Master's degree graduation, May 2021)

Conclusion

Reading the stories of undocumented immigrants and refugees gives us the opportunity to better understand the many reasons why they had to migrate to this country. Some of those reasons had to do with the United States direct involvement in Latin America that led to Civil Wars or the destruction of their economic systems. By understanding their challenges, hopefully you will be better educated when engaging with others on the issue of migration from Latin America. The idea that individuals should just stay in the back of the line, when there is no line to follow, makes absolutely no sense. Years ago, the United States eliminated the registry law that allowed individuals to seek immigration status after having resided in the United States for seven years. Since this law doesn't exist at the moment and Congress refuses to approve the reinstatement of it, individuals like the ones in this book have no other option but to live here without status.

Every single one of the individuals that shared their story has at least a bachelor's degree and a few of them have masters degrees. Our intention is not to highlight and promote the idea that those who obtain college diplomas should get an opportunity to gain status in the United States. We recognize that every single individual who migrates to this country, regardless of the reason, has unique challenges that they must face and as a result of this, not everybody should be expected to get a college diploma. We need doctors as much as we need plumbers. We need teachers and school counselors as much as we need bakers. Many undocumented immigrants and refugees who live in this country harvest the grapes, work construction, babysit children of US citizens and in general, do work that most citizens do not want to do.

While we could write multiple volumes on some of the over 300 DACA recipients that we have supported for over 10 years, we wanted to share a glimpse into their experiences, traumas, and successes. We need to do away with the erroneous idea of the good immigrant. Even immigrants and refugees have fallen victims to this idea that some deserve to gain legal status by being perfect. This refers to obtaining a college diploma, never getting a speeding ticket, and assimilating to the cultural values, beliefs, and norms of this country. The reality is that the best these individuals can do is acculturate because as long as their skin tone is dark, whether they end up as US citizens, they will always be seen as the other. We hope that this book will be shared with family and friends and that it becomes a conversation starter about the issue of migration and why we should create a welcoming system for those who had to leave everything they had in order to improve their lives.

We also hope that undocumented individuals will read this book and be motivated to continue to move forward in their education, employment, and civic participation. We cannot allow the lack of a nine-digit social security number to limit the level of success that these individuals can achieve. We cannot allow the lack of access to a social security number to prevent these individuals from contributing to the economy and the overall success of this country. We hope that this book has been of use to you and that you will share the knowledge that you have obtained with as many people as possible. It is not until we take the time to get to know other individuals, that we can finally begin to understand them.

Rafael Vázquez Guzmán
CEO, Líderes del Futuro Avanzando
(Future Leaders Moving Forward)

Made in the USA
Columbia, SC
29 July 2024